INSIGHT COMPACT GUIDES

H a w a i i
Maui

Compact Guide: Maui is the ultimate quick-reference guide to this most varied of Hawaiian islands. It tells you all you need to know about Maui's attractions, from the bustling resorts of West Maui to the historical charms of Lahaina, from the sweeping Hana Coast to the soaring heights of Haleakala.

This is one of more than 80 titles in *Apa Publications'* new series of pocket-sized, easy-to-use guidebooks intended for the independent-minded traveler. *Compact Guides* are in essence travel encyclopedias in miniature, designed to be comprehensive yet portable, as well as up-to-date and authoritative.

Star Attractions

An instant reference to some of Maui's top attractions to help you set your priorities.

Ka'anapali p17

Lahaina p20

'Iao Valley p33

Ho'okipa Beach p37

Upcountry p38

Haleakala p43

Hana Coast p50

Hana p53

'Ohe'o Gulch p55

Molokai p57

Upcounry Protea p39

Hawaii

Maui

Introduction

Places

Culture

Leisure

Practical Information

Maui – The Best of Everything

Maui and the islands of Hawaii – said to be the most remote island group on the planet – leave little to the imagination, except for those travelers who've yet to visit. For them, the mind can run amuck with idyllic images of beaches, aquamarine water, rain forests and aloha spirit. What people don't anticipate is a place with one of the most diverse geographies imaginable, as is its population that is 60 percent Asian or Pacific Islander, often speaking a medley of languages and with no single racial or cultural group a majority.

Beaches and aquamarine water

The quality of life in Hawaii is perhaps America's best, with the lowest death rates from disease and cancer, and the healthiest population. Many Hawaii residents would say that Maui, of all the main islands, has the best of everything in the islands: mountains and coastline among the best in the Pacific, and with just enough people (around 100,000) to create the critical mass necessary to nurture cultural pursuits and a robust night life. In many ways, Maui is blessed in that over 80 percent of Hawaii's 1.2 million residents live on a different island – Oahu – which includes the state's only metropolis, Honolulu, America's 11th-largest city. This reason alone makes Maui the island of choice for many, although those who have chosen Maui over Oahu seeking to escape traffic and housing congestion have, in fact, introduced them to Maui.

5

Rugged terrain

Location and geography

Popular belief deposits Hawaii in the South Pacific, which is quite wrong. Hawaii is 1,500 miles (2,400km) north of the equator and on the same latitude as Mexico City, Bombay and Hong Kong. Yet without a map, one could understandably imagine the Hawaiian islands as nestled in the South Pacific, as the islands are indeed part of Polynesia, as is Tahiti, which *is* in the South Pacific. True, Hawaii is mostly tropical, yet it also has an astonishing range of climates and terrain, including rain forests, deserts, temperate zones and tundra regions. It even snows in Hawaii, occasionally on Maui's Haleakala and always each winter on the Big Island, where glaciers once existed.

Maui is the second-largest of Hawaii's 130-plus islands and shoals that extend 1,500 miles (2,400km) from the Big Island northwest to Kure Atoll. In land area, Hawaii is America's fourth-smallest state, with the Big Island (4,000 sq miles/10,400 sq km) alone three times as large as the smallest state of Rhode Island. Maui covers 730 square miles (1,900 sq km), followed in size by Oahu, Kauai, Molokai, Lanai and Niʻihau. The 130

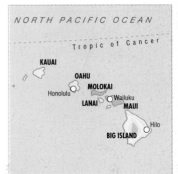

NORTH PACIFIC OCEAN

Tropic of Cancer

KAUAI

OAHU

MOLOKAI

Honolulu

LANAI

Wailuku

MAUI

Hilo

BIG ISLAND

West Maui heights

Upcountry mists

Makena Beach

or so uninhabited islands in the chain contain a total of only 3 sq miles (8 sq km), and with the exception of Midway, all are part of the State of Hawaii. Politically, the state is divided into four counties: Hawaii (the Big Island), Maui (including Molokai, Lanai, Kaho'olawe), Kauai (including Ni'ihau), and the City and County of Honolulu, which includes not only Oahu but all of those uninhabited atolls and islands. Each county is governed by a mayor, with a governor and lieutenant governor heading the state's executive branch.

Island formation

Maui, like the other Hawaiian islands, sits atop a tectonic plate, moving slowly to the northwest. There is a stationary hot spot more than 50 miles (80km) deep in the earth's mantle. As the tectonic plate has passed over this hot spot, from southeast to northwest, over 80 volcanoes have risen to form the Hawaiian Ridge – and islands – during the past 44 million years. Each emerged volcano eventually ceased activity as the plate moved away from the hot spot. Another volcano and island then formed. (This fact of island formation is accurately reflected in the centuries-old legend of Pele, the fire goddess who frequently changed homes in Hawaii.)

Maui slipped off the hotspot within the last two centuries, and now only the Big Island remains volcanically active, while the oldest islands to the northwest have eroded until there is little, if anything, remaining above water. Many of the uninhabited 'islands' are in fact nothing more than coral atolls; everything else has long since eroded away or collapsed. One day, too, Maui and all the other Hawaiian islands will erode away.

The volcanoes grew slowly and methodically, adding shallow layer upon layer to make what are called shield volcanoes. From afar, the gently arching contours of an above-water shield volcano betray its mass and height: Haleakala, and thus most of Maui, is thought by some geologists to be the most massive single mountain on earth. The highest point on Haleakala is 10, 023ft (3,055m) above sea level, but at one time, when Maui was an adolescent, it was nearly 14,000ft (4,200m) high, higher even than the Big Island is today. West Maui, the smaller western peninsula of the island, is also a volcano, older and considerably lower than Haleakala. The two peninsulas are joined by a valley-like isthmus, which has earned Maui the nickname of the 'valley isle'.

Flora and fauna

The first vegetation to take root in Hawaii arrived, like the first people, on Pacific currents. Statistically, new species were established on the islands every 15,000 years. They evolved with no protection against predators, as there were none. Evolution proceeded in blissful isolation, producing nearly 9,000 kinds of flora and fauna unique to Hawaii.

Mammals were even less likely to drift ashore in those early millennia, and there are only two native mammals: the Hawaiian monk seal, now endangered, and the hoary bat. A third species inadvertently carried to Hawaii aboard early Polynesian canoes, the Polynesian rat, is considered to have evolved on Hawaii into a unique subspecies.

The Polynesians introduced pigs, fowl and dogs to Hawaii, along with bamboo, ginger, taro, guava, banana, sweet potato, coconut, sugar cane and hibiscus. Europeans introduced goats, cattle and numerous rodents and birds (and alien human viruses). With no natural defenses against mammals or competing flora, indigenous plants were often ravaged into extinction; those remaining in Hawaii today exist in remote and inaccessible areas.

Local plumage

Whales

The Hawaiian islands are a winter refuge for humpback whales, especially in the protected waters off Maui, sheltered by the neighboring islands of Molokai, Lanai and Kaho'olawe. They stay from around November to April to mate, give birth and nurture newborn; the waters around Hawaii are much warmer than the Alaskan waters where the whales spend their summers.

The ancient Hawaiians observed whales during their annual winter migrations to the islands, but as whale meat was not a source of food in pre-contact times, the Hawaiians left the whales alone. It wasn't until the early 1800s, when New England whalers ventured into the Pacific, that Hawaii took on importance in whaling, not for the whales themselves, but for Hawaii's strategic location that allowed the whaling ships to operate in the Pacific. The sperm whale was the most sought-after species, with excellent oil for use in oil lamps and as lubrication. Whaling's importance in Hawaii lasted about 40 years, peaking in the 1840s. Lahaina took on considerable importance as an anchorage during the peak years, with Honolulu temporarily taking a back seat.

Humpback whales are from 10 to 15ft (3.5–4.5m) long at birth, weighing 1 to 3 tons. As they nurse, newborn gain 200 pounds (90kg) a day. When adult, they can average 45ft (14m) long and 40 tons in weight. On average, about 600 humpback whales show up in Hawaii; some experts say that this is but a small fraction of the number a century or two ago. Whales are now protected by both federal and state laws.

Also protected in Hawaiian waters are sea turtles, including green, hawksbill and leatherback. Known as *honu,* turtles live up to 100 years.

Humpbacks whales are protected

People and population

The Native Hawaiian population in 1778 was estimated at around 300,000. Eleven decades later, when the monarchy was overthrown, it stood at 40,000, and many of those were *hapa*, or part, Hawaiian. Not only did the population decline, but so too the Hawaiians' morale. Europeans noted the change in less than 50 years from a hard-working and diligent people to one with no spirit. *Na kanaka kuu wale aku no I ka uhane...* The people freely gave up their souls and died. According to state statistics, there are less than 10,000 full-blooded Hawaiians today.

Time for reflection

By the mid-19th century, when sugar became a powerful commodity, plantations started importing labor. (With the exception of whites, most non-Hawaiian groups initially arrived in the islands as plantation laborers.) The first contract workers from China arrived in the early 1850s, followed over the next six decades by laborers from Japan, Portugal, Korea and the Philippines. Significant numbers stayed when their contracts finished.

Since the first Western contact, the make-up of Hawaii's population is shifting from Hawaiian to Asian to Caucasian. Indeed, with 23 percent, whites (*haole*, lit. having no breath) have replaced Japanese (22 percent) as the largest minority group. They are followed by Filipinos (15 percent), then Chinese, blacks (not necessarily from the US), Koreans and Samoans. Vietnamese and Laotians are the most recent arrivals. These statistics only give part of the story, however, for they don't reflect the large percentage of interracial marriages in Hawaii. Around 30 percent of residents claim Catholicism, 20 percent Buddhism, and 10 percent Protestantism.

The two main crops: sugar cane and pineapples

Economy

Human society in Hawaii has always distilled down to control of land. The first wave of Polynesians from the Marquesas Islands found the islands uninhabited, and thus inhabitable in their own image. Centuries later, Polynesians from Tahiti had to subdue the earlier Marquesans before settling down in Hawaii. Europeans and Americans followed later, doing likewise in their own way.

Pre-contact Hawaiian society was aristocratic and feudal. Ideally, a chief held the land in trust for the gods, assigning its administration to *ali'i*, the aristocrats that gave him support. After 1778, with the introduction of Western market values, a dual economy developed over several decades. Increasingly, however, international market forces dominated Hawaii's economy, forcing a fundamental shift in society. As Hawaii's economic role in the world increased, haole families, many of them descendants of early missionaries, gained control over much of Hawaii's usable land, a situation that persists today.

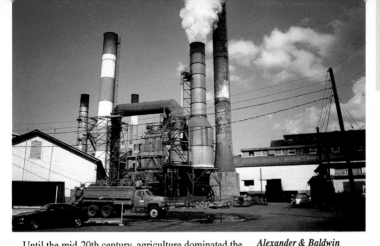

Until the mid-20th century, agriculture dominated the economy. Then World War II introduced a large number of visitors of a different kind. After the war, these soldiers and sailors returned home with fond memories, and when commercial jets made access to the islands easy a decade and a half later, the word about Hawaii was already spreading. Today, tourism is by far the most important aspect of Hawaii's economy, with over six million visitors annually, and Maui is the second most popular destination after Oahu. Next in economic importance is the military, although there is virtually no military presence on Maui. Agriculture, increasingly a distant third place in the state, is still a significant economic force on Maui, where both the central isthmus and West Maui are dominated by sugar cane and pineapples.

Alexander & Baldwin sugar processing plant

9

More modern, hotel architecture

Language and orientation

A potpourri of languages drift on Hawaii's trade winds, but English is the common and unifying language. Initially confounding to visitors are words that may sound like English, but somehow not. Pidgin English is a local approach to talking story, or having a conversation. As different ethnic groups came together to work on plantations, pidgin borrowed from all and became the common lingo.

Conversational English is also sprinkled with words from Hawaiian, such as in 'I'm *pau,*' or 'I'm finished'. *Aloha,* of course, is hello, good-bye and love. *Mahalo,* thank you. *Kama'aina* is a local resident, while a *malihini* is a newcomer. Others to know: *kokua,* help; *kapu,* forbidden; *ali'i,* royalty; *ohana,* family; *keiki,* child(ren).

On all islands, *mauka* means towards the mountains, while *makai* indicates on the ocean side. 'It's *makai* of the road', for example. It's an extremely functional method of orientation, more useful than the compass points, and so we use these terms in this guide.

Historical Highlights

1.3–1.15 million BC The West Maui volcano begins its rise above the Pacific Ocean. Half a million years later, Haleakala surfaces, eventually reaching nearly 15,000ft (4,500m) above sea level.

AD 300–500 Perhaps seeking refuge from domestic turmoil or population pressures, the first group of Polynesians from the Marquesas, 2,500 miles (4,000km) to the south, discover the uninhabited Hawaiian islands. After over six centuries of isolation, they are replaced or assimilated by newly arrived Tahitians.

c1750 Kamehameha the Great is born on the Big Island.

1778 The native population is estimated at over a quarter of a million people. Apparently the first European contact, English explorer Captain James Cook arrives in the islands, naming them the Sandwich Islands, after the Earl of Sandwich, one of his strongest supporters in England.

1779 Initially welcomed as an incarnation of the god Lono, the now-mortal Captain Cook is killed on the Big Island in a dispute with disillusioned Hawaiians; his two ships, *HMS Discovery* and *HMS Resolute*, continue on to Oahu.

1786 Western ships accidentally discover 58-acre (23 hectares) Necker Island, in the northwestern part of the island chain, only to find evidence of pre-contact Polynesian habitation.

1790 The last volcanic eruption on Maui takes place on Haleakala's lower southwest flank. Kamehameha the Great, having unified the Big Island, begins his conquest of the neighboring islands. Assisted by cannon borrowed from Europeans, a decisive battle in 'Iao Valley gives Kamehameha control over Maui. Five years later, Kamehameha conquers Oahu. Kauai and Ni'ihau, however, don't yield to his force, but choose to join Kamehameha's union in 1810.

1819 Kamehameha the Great dies. Shortly afterwards, his favorite wife, Maui-born Ka'ahumanu, and son abolish the taboo of men and women eating together, effectively forcing the collapse of traditional Hawaiian society.

1820 The kingdom's capital and royal court is moved to Lahaina, on Maui. Protestant missionaries from New England arrive and are swiftly offended by Hawaiian culture. The native population is estimated at 130,000, half that of 1778.

1840 Whaling reaches its peak, especially on Maui, which temporarily eclipses Oahu in importance. Hawaii's first constitution is introduced by Kamehameha III, but the sovereignty of the monarchy is challenged by the resident British consul who, aided by a gunboat, forces Kamehameha III to cede Hawaii to Queen Victoria. Displeased, Victoria extends apologies, and Hawaii's sovereignty is recognized.

1845 Hawaii's capital returned to Honolulu from Lahaina.

1848 The Great Mahele (Land Division) signals a change in Hawaiian attitudes regarding land, shifting towards a more Western approach. The Great Mahele divides the possession and control of land in Hawaii amongst the monarchy, *ali'i* and the government, and, two years later, to individuals, including foreigners.

1852 Faced with a Hawaiian work force whose morale and interest in field labor has declined, plantations start importing Chinese laborers.

1866 The first leprosy patients are forced into isolated exile on Molokai, at Kalaupapa. Seven years later, Father Damien arrives to care for patients, dying in 1889 of contracted leprosy.

1868 Sugar planters start importing laborers from Japan.

1876 A reciprocity treaty between Hawaii and the United States allows products from Hawaii – especially sugar – to enter the United States duty-free. As trade between the US and Hawaii is mostly one-way, Hawaii benefits considerably from the treaty, and sugar starts to dominate Hawaii's economy and politics.

1887 Hawaii's geographical importance has long been recognized by mariners, especially for taking on provisions and water. Now, sailing ships are replaced by steam-powered vessels, and the United States, claiming that Hawaii could be an important stop for its expanding naval fleet, gains rights to use Pearl Harbor as a coal station.

1891 King Kalakaua, who both revived Hawaiian culture and embraced Western ways, dies. Lili'uokalani ascends to the throne as queen.

1893 The Kingdom of Hawaii is by now recognized as a sovereign nation by most of the Western world, including the United States. Nevertheless, Queen Lili'uokalani is overthrown by American businessmen, with the help of US Marines. She yields the islands peacefully, believing that the illegal coup will be recognized as such, and the islands returned to the monarchy. Pres. Grover Cleveland pleads that the overthrow of the Hawaiian monarchy – the 'lawless occupation of Honolulu under false pretenses by the United States forces' – must be denied and the monarchy restored. Congress, however, refuses to condemn the overthrow. Lili'uokalani takes up exile in her Honolulu home, where she remains until her death in 1917.

1894 The United States recognizes the new Republic of Hawaii, with Sanford Dole as its president. A year later, *kama'aina* Robert Wilcox initiates an unsuccessful counter-coup to restore the Hawaiian monarchy.

1898 The United States formally annexes Hawaii.

1900 Hawaii is made a territory of the United States. All of the land ceded to the Hawaiian government and monarchy under the Great Mahele of 1848 is now transferred to federal control.

1901 Lahaina's Pioneer Inn opens, and for decades is the only accommodation on Maui.

1903 The first pineapple cannery in Hawaii is opened, and cultivation begins in earnest.

1909 The Hawaiian Islands National Wildlife Refuge is established by President Teddy Roosevelt, protecting most of Hawaii's northwestern, uninhabited islands. Sugar planters start importing laborers from the Philippines.

1916 Haleakala is incorporated into the Big Island's Hawaii Volcanoes National Park; in 1961, it is established as a separate national park.

1929 Interisland air service starts, followed in 1936 by the China Clippers, which stop in Hawaii during trans-Pacific flights from North America to Asia.

1941 Japan attacks Pearl Harbor, bringing the United States into World War II. Maui escapes attack, but for the duration of the war, Hawaii is placed under martial law and administered by the military. Civil rights are suspended.

1946 Sugar workers hold a two-month strike, gaining higher pay and fewer hours of work, but clipping the paternal connections with plantation owners.

1959 After a public vote, Hawaiians choose to become America's 50th state. Commercial jet service is begun to Hawaii from the mainland, making Hawaii easily accessible to holiday visitors. The pineapple industry peaks.

1974 George Ariyoshi becomes the first Japanese-American governor in America.

1978 The last regularly-scheduled American-flag passenger ship between the US mainland and Hawaii arrives.

1986 Hawaii's first ethnically-Hawaiian governor, John Waihee, takes office.

1989 Japanese investment in Hawaii real estate reaches US$7.3 billion. As the Japanese economy superheats, yen investment in both residential and commercial property in Hawaii drives up property prices – and property taxes – to inflated values. Japanese investors purchase numerous hotels and spend millions of dollars renovating them.

1990 Hawaii's population exceeds one million, of which Maui has just over 100,000.

1993 100th anniversary of the Hawaiian monarchy's overthrow pushes debate about Hawaiian sovereignty to the foreground. Shortly after a vacation in Hawaii, President Bill Clinton signs a joint Congressional resolution that acknowledges the illegitimacy of the annexation in 1898, and apologizes to the Native Hawaiian people.

1994 Filipino-American Ben Cayetano is elected governor.

Ka'anapali Resort

Tour 1

West Maui

*Preceding pages:
a windsurfer's paradise*

The rugged eastern coast

Odds are that anybody going to Maui goes to West Maui, the smaller half of the island. It's also the older half, with the volcano that created West Maui now carved into exquisite valleys and pinnacles. These mountains of the old volcano also create a rain shadow, extracting most of the moisture from the northeasterly trade winds, leaving little rain for the other side. Thus, the western coast of West Maui – Lahaina and Ka'anapali – is dry and sunny, and seductive for mainlanders weary of winter snow and gloom. (Maui's other dry coast is that of Kihei and Wailea, in the rain shadow of Haleakala.)

But with this seduction of travelers comes development, and traffic snarls, and large resorts. Most of this development is confined to a 10-mile (16km) stretch between Lahaina and Kapalua. Yet, not far away, on West Maui's eastern coast, is some of Maui's most rugged terrain, and in between, in the mountains, some of Hawaii's most idyllic landscape. This tour confines itself largely to the coast; those wishing to see the impressive 'Iao Valley, should follow Tour 3 from Wailuku (*see pages 32–3*).

From Kahului International Airport, Route 38 heads southwest towards the southern side of the central isthmus connecting West Maui with Haleakala, meeting up with Route 30, the Honoapi'ilani Highway. An alternative route is to follow Route 340 up the eastern coast of West Maui, then down into Kapalua and Ka'anapali. Indeed, the only significant road on West Maui is the one that completely circles the central West Maui Mountains, what remains of the old West Maui volcano.

On the southern shore of the central isthmus, **Ma'alaea** serves up little except excursion boats and a restaurant, but **Ma'alaea Bay** offers prime whale-watching from November through April. This wonderful fact makes driving the southern road up towards Lahaina problematic, as rental cars screech irrationally and without much forethought to a stop when a whale spouts offshore. Designated by an act of Congress in 1992, the **Hawaiian Islands Humpback Whale National Marine Sanctuary** protects the reproductive and birthing activities of whales in Hawaii. Extending from the ocean's high-water mark to depths of 600ft (180m), the sanctuary includes waters surrounding Maui, Lanai, Kaha'alowe and Molokai, as well as the waters adjacent to Kauai's Kilauea National Wildlife Refuge.

Whale-watching excursion

For countless centuries, humpback whales have used these waters as a winter refuge for rest and birthing. But in the past decade or so, the whales have found themselves the center of attention, drawing motorized boats out to where they relax and nurse. Despite what whale-watching boat operators might claim, many of their operations are highly intrusive during the winter migration period, even though federal and state laws forbid boats from approaching closer than 300ft (90m), or helicopters lower

15

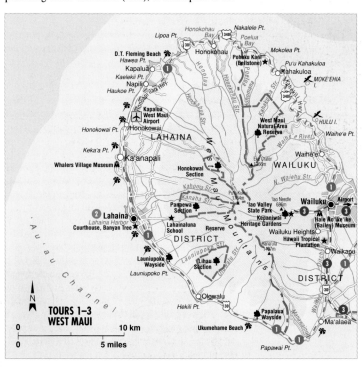

than 1,000ft (300m). While being able to witness these wondrous mammals up close increases public appreciation of them, there's something even more special about letting them be in peace. Watch from dry land, after pulling off the road at **Papawai Point**, or buy a video (there are dozens of them).

Hugging the coastline, Route 30 passes through a short tunnel on its way towards **Olowalu**, a blink-the-eyes-and-it's-history roadside stop, with a traditional general store, restaurant, the ruins of a sugar mill, and a little bit of history. A little way *mauka* up a dirt road behind Olowalu are **petroglyphs** etched into a cliff face. Inland, an ancient trail once paralleled Olowalu Stream, climbing the 5,000-ft (1,500m) slopes of the West Maui Mountains, over the ancient caldera's lip and into 'Iao Valley (*see Tour 3, page 33*). During the 1790 Battle of 'Iao Valley, where Kamehameha the Great defeated the Mauian army, the Maui chief escaped over the West Maui Mountains to Olowalu using the old trail; he later met Kamehameha again, on Oahu, and again in defeat. Also in 1790, over 100 Hawaiians were killed here in an ambush by the captain of an American ship. Earlier, one of his sailors and a small launch had gone missing. Simon Metcalfe, the captain, invited Hawaiians to his ship for trading, and when they arrived, opened fire on them.

Petroglyphs near Olowalu

North of Olowalu, West Maui starts getting urban on the *makai* side of the road. On the *mauka* side, towards the mountains, the lower slopes are softened by blankets of sugar cane and pineapple, punctuated by large hills of stones cleared from the soil.

Lahaina entices artists

Twenty-two miles (35km) from Kahului, ★★ **Lahaina**, of course, is where all travelers since Europeans found Hawaii have stopped. Front Street, the prime road of this one-time whaling town and now a contemporary tourist trap, still retains some of its 19th-century textures, although increasingly one must look hard through the loud commercialism. (For details, *see Tour 2, page 20.*) Marking the turnoff – Lahainaluna Road – from Route 30 into central Lahaina is the old **Pioneer Sugar Mill**, first built in the early 1870s and *mauka* of the road, announced by its tall and tired smokestack. Lahainaluna Road leads directly to the harbor and Front Street.

Just north of the sugar mill is the terminal station for the 1890s-era sugar-cane train, the **Lahaina-Ka'anapali Pacific Railroad**, which runs hourly 6 miles (10km) one-way between Lahaina and Ka'anapali through cane fields and, yes, golf courses. Although unquestionably a tourist ploy, this narrow-gauge train is authentic and follows the rail bed once used by the Pioneer Mill until the early 1950s. Open-air cars snake behind the smoke-shooting steam

locomotive, accompanied for better or worse by a 'ukulele-playing – and singing – conductor. The trip takes about half an hour.

Ka'anapali: for surfing…

Three miles north of Lahaina, ★★ **Ka'anapali**, Hawaii's first planned resort – and still its largest, although only half of it is actually developed – was nothing but scrub-covered land four decades ago. Planning for the resort began during the 1950s, in a flash of entrepreneurial insight that anticipated the tourist-drawing power of a jet-age Hawaii. More than anything else on the island, including its natural wonders such as Haleakala, Ka'anapali turned agricultural Maui into the state's second-most popular visitor destination.

strolling…

17

Luxury hotels, exquisite condominiums, an ever-enlarging shopping center, and the requisite golf courses are well integrated with one another in Ka'anapali. Three-mile-long **Ka'anapali Beach** links it all together, lined by wonderful sand and a well-traveled walkway. The Hyatt Regency Maui, at the southern end of the beach, is the standard by which most other 'fantasy resorts' have been measured in Hawaii. Once there were hotels, then resorts, and finally fantasy mega-resorts, pioneered here by developer Chris Hemmeter. Some of his properties, such as the Hyatt Maui, were done quite well, with exquisite antiques and art gracing hotel grounds. Others, as in Waikoloa on the Big Island, were ridiculously over-the-top, with fake canal boats and electric trams, more Disneyworld than Hawaii.

… and sailing

At the other end of the main beach is the Sheraton Maui, at **Black Rock**. Built in 1963 (and thoroughly renovated in 1996), this was the first hotel in Ka'anapali. Black Rock, or **Pu'u Keka'a**, was the focus of Hawaiian life for a thousand years, and Ka'anapali an ancient capital of Maui and long a retreat of *ali'i*. Kamehameha the Great had an enor-

Snorkelling is another option

mous *heiau* built near Pu'u Keka'a, although it no longer exists. Pu'u Keka'a was one of Hawaii's *'uhane lele* – a sacred spot from which the souls of the dead departed for the spirit world.

As with Waikiki, some visitors retreat to Ka'anapali and never leave its confines. An adventure for them is walking from one hotel to the next. Like Waikiki, this is not a Hawaiian experience, and you have been warned. Still, the pleasures of Ka'anapali are abundant – food at beachfront restaurants, some of Hawaii's best weather, offshore diversions like snorkeling and sailing, daydreaming or staring at nearby Molokai, seemingly close enough to hurl sand at.

The beachside restaurants of ★ **Whaler's Village** (shops daily 9am–10pm, restaurants to 2am) start to fill as sundown approaches. Besides nearly 50 shops and restaurants, Whaler's Village has a 40ft-long (12m) sperm-whale skeleton. Two whaling museums, both of them free and well worth the time, are the **Whale Center of the Pacific** (9.30am–10pm), which chronicles the commercial aspects of 19th-century whaling, and **Hale Kohola** (House of the Whale), which explores the natural history and physiology of the ocean's many whale species.

Further north, accommodations continue, although ambiance doesn't. The vaguely-defined towns of **Honokowai**, **Kahana** and **Napili** are known for their affordable rental condominiums, but little else, including few decent beaches. Napili in particular gets trashed a lot by many, but like Kihei, it allows many visitors an affordable vacation. Unless staying along here, there's absolutely no reason under the sun to venture off the main highway, unless going up towards the mountains, where the **Kapalua West Maui Airport** offers connecting commuter flights to Honolulu.

Sperm-whale skeleton at Whaler's Village

Napili butts up against ★★ **Kapalua**, a different world from its southern neighbors. Kapalua has its pineapples, but it is the exquisite accommodations (Kapalua Bay Hotel and Villas, along with the Ritz-Carlton), wine-tasting and golf that give it a gold-card caché. It is an extremely quiet place, accessed from the main highway on Hawaii's worst-named avenue, especially in a resort – Office Road. Down below, a crescent of golden sand, **Kapalua Beach**, is often considered to be one of the most perfect beaches in the United States. We can think of other candidates in Hawaii, actually, but Kapalua is quite good. (Access to the beach is from a parking lot near Kapalua Bay Hotel.) Less subjectively, Kapalua's three golf courses are consistently rated as some of America's finest. In summer, Kapalua is host to two world-renowned events, the Kapalua Music Festival and the Kapalua Wine Symposium. Although the resort dominates Kapalua, over 20,000 acres (8,000 hectares) of pineapple are still grown on the surrounding land. (During construction of the Ritz-Carlton, an ancient burial site with hundreds of bodies was uncovered; the hotel was relocated somewhat inland.)

Beyond Kapalua, Route 30 tips out near Lipoa Point, then parallels a spectacular coastline to **Honokohau Bay**, 5 miles (8km) from Kapalua and at the mouth of West Maui's longest stream. At the head of Honokohau Valley – near West Maui's tallest point, **Pu'u Kukui** (5,788 ft/1,764m) – is Honokohau Falls, one of the world's highest waterfalls, 1,120ft (340m) high and inaccessible by foot. The highway, meanwhile, continues onwards, climbing up from the bay through agricultural land lined by ironwood trees. **Nakalele Point**, West Maui's northern tip, is bare basalt and with cliffs vulnerable to the elements.

The terrain south of Nakalele competes with Kaupo, on Maui's southern coast, for remoteness and road-driving challenges. From here, the east coast of West Maui is mostly ranch land, with coastlines of steep cliffs, blowholes and tempestuous waves.

Near **Kahakuloa**, 8 miles (13km) from Honokohau Bay, the road narrows to one lane and follows steep cliffs along the sea; pay attention to traffic ahead, and yield rather than insisting on the right of way. Kahakuloa (lit. the tall lord) is both the name of a small village, and of a 640-ft-high (200m) volcanic dome that dominates the mouth of the small valley emptying into the ocean. Directly south of it is 550-ft (170m) **Pu'u Kahuli'anapa**, another volcanic dome.

South of Kahakuloa, Route 340 continues its convoluted way, climbing inland somewhat before eventually unwinding on the alluvial plain of the 'Iao Stream, and into downtown Wailuku, 15 miles (24km) from the solitude of Kahakuloa.

Kapalua pineapples

Kids at Kapalua Beach

Lahaina's own Bud the Birdman

Tour 2

Lahaina

With a modest population of 10,000 residents, Lahaina is one of those places straddling kitsch and authenticity at the same time, and never knowing which way to tumble. For decades, local preservation groups have encouraged, successfully for the most part, the preservation of the town's older buildings; Lahaina was designated a National Historic District in 1962. But an incredible amount of tourist schlock is offered in its stores, not to mention a Hard Rock Cafe and a Planet Hollywood. Lahaina is a certified tourist ambush, increasingly contrived in the same way that, say, Key West is contrived.

But, having said that, like Key West, Lahaina has its substantive history and its see-and-be-seen ambiance, and it's a fun place to hang out. Few have regrets about time spent here. It's not a very big place; eventually, find a place to put your feet up at sundown and people-watch.

For nearly two centuries Lahaina has drawn an eclectic crowd of monarchs, misfits, missionaries, mariners and mongrels – and tourists – to its streets. The relationships

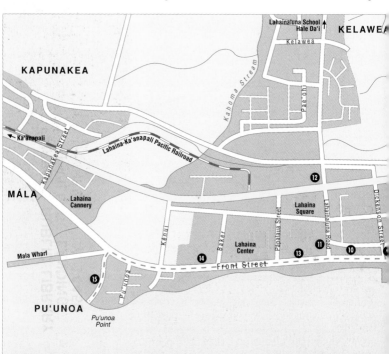

between groups have not always been of brotherhood and harmony, particularly between the Protestant missionaries and warped sailors too long at sea.

From 1820 until 1845, Lahaina was capital of the Hawaiian kingdom. This alone, however, did not impart momentum on the small town. Rather, it was whaling that gave Lahaina its critical mass. Whalers started venturing to Hawaii in the early 1800s, sailing their ships around Cape Horn from New England in search of sperm-whale oil, used for lamps and lubrication. And when sperm whales became difficult to find, then bowhead, gray, right and humpback whales were hunted. Commercial whaling peaked in the mid-1840s, when over 400 ships annually would drop anchor off Lahaina, which then had about 3,500 residents, along with 530 dogs, according to a census by missionaries. Rowdy Lahaina began to fizzle in the late 1850s, as the trade in whale oil was replaced by newly-discovered Pennsylvania crude.

Herman Melville, author of the whaling classic *Moby Dick*, sought work in Lahaina, but failing there, he shipped off to Honolulu to work as a store clerk and then a pin setter in a bowling alley. Saturated with whaling ambiance, Melville returned to Boston to become a writer. He never returned to the Pacific.

There she blows!

21

Today's catches are smaller

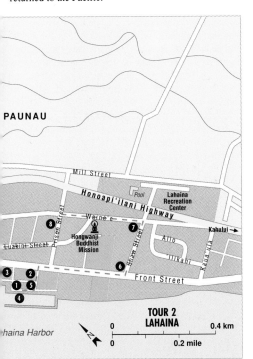

PAUNAU

Mill Street

Honoapi'ilani Highway

Pool

Lahaina Recreation Center

We'ine'e

Hongwanji Buddhist Mission

Aho

Ilikahi

Kahului →

Front Street

haina Harbor

TOUR 2 LAHAINA

0   0.4 km

0   0.2 mile

A good place to start a rowdy Lahaina ramble of our own is along the waterfront, at **Lahaina Harbor**, where whalers have been replaced by deep-sea fishing boats filled with chests of cold beer. Facing the small harbor is the ★ **Old Courthouse ❶**, a humble building on Wharf Street that was once both customhouse and courthouse. It was here, in 1898, that the Hawaiian flag was replaced by the American flag in the official annexation ceremony.

The Lahaina Arts Society operates two galleries (9am–5pm) within the courthouse: the **Old Jail Gallery** and **Banyan Tree Gallery**, both exhibiting artists of Maui. The basement-level Old Jail Gallery was, in fact, once the town's jail. There is also a **visitors center** (daily 9am–5pm) for tourists on the first floor, offering good, helpful information about both Lahaina and Maui.

The stones of the courthouse come from an earlier courthouse, Hale Piula (lit. iron-roof house), which once stood nearby. Built in the 1830s, Hale Piula was intended to be a palace for Kamehameha III, who fancied instead a small and less embellished hut nearby, and so never occupied the palace. It became a courthouse, until a storm greatly damaged it in the late 1850s, and its stones were salvaged for the present edifice.

Romance under the Banyan Tree

Behind the courthouse, directly *mauka* or towards the mountains, is the ★ **Banyan Tree ❷**, which, if overlooked, suggests a trip to the optician. This is a *huge* tree, not because of its 60ft (20m) height, but for its wandering branches – supported by both secondary trunks and artificial supports because of the weight – shading two-thirds of an acre. Brought over from India, but only 8ft (2.5m) tall at the time, the tree was planted by the sheriff of Lahaina in the early 1870s to commemorate the 50th anniversary of Protestant missionaries in Lahaina.

Pioneer Inn

Across the street, unmistakable with its green-and-white facade, the ★ **Pioneer Inn ❸** was, for a long time after its opening in 1901, until the late 1950s, the only accommodation in West Maui. The original section of the hotel faces the harbor; additional rooms and spaces for shops were added in the 1960s, following the original design. An effort has been made to upgrade the place recently, installing air conditioning and televisions, and spiffing up the trim. Some of its 45 rooms, however, are less than quiet, as there is a popular bar downstairs that stays open quite late. Still, the Pioneer Inn is real, and economical, and deliciously convenient to the waterfront.

Always mentioned in guide books but with nothing to see is the long-gone (since the 1950s) taro patch – once growing next to the hotel – said to have been worked by Kamehameha III as a living example of industry for his subjects. Closer to the water and visible are the remnants of the so-called **Brick Palace**, constructed around 1800 and probably the first western-style building in Hawaii. Two British ex-convicts, fresh from serving time at Botany Bay, in Australia, built the palace at the request of Kamehameha the Great, who intended it for Ka'ahumanu, his favorite wife. Buoyed by his conquest of Maui, Kamehameha himself used the simple two-story building in 1802 to plot his invasion of still-unconquered Kauai, his fleet of war canoes assembling off Lahaina. (Kauai never yielded militarily to Kamehameha; it joined Kamehameha's united Hawaiian islands by agreement, in 1810.) By the mid-19th century, after serving as a residence and storehouse, it fell derelict. Its foundations and the cornerstones, however, are preserved in the grassy area between the Pioneer Inn and harbor.

Carthaginian II

Impossible to overlook is the 90-ft (30m) ★ *Carthaginian II* ❹ (daily 10am–4.30pm), a restored, 19th-century square-rigged brig, said to be the only of its kind remaining anywhere. Fast sailing ships of this type introduced commerce to Hawaii. It's the second Carthaginian, actually, because the first one sank off Lahaina in the 1970s, on its way for a refit in Honolulu; this replacement was brought from Denmark. *Carthaginian II* includes exhibits on whaling, and there is an original whaleboat of that era found in Alaska and returned to Maui in the 1970s.

23

Next to the Old Courthouse and banyan tree, at the intersection of Wharf and Canal streets, is the reconstructed corner wall of an **old fort** ❺, dating from the 1830s. Building the fort was in response to the cannonballs that furious seamen on whaling ships at anchor offshore fired at the missionary compound in Lahaina. Earlier, disgusted by the 'hell-hole' that Lahaina had become, missionaries initiated a law that forbade Hawaiian women from swimming out to personally greet arriving ships and their crews. The cannonballs did little, however, but kick up

The old fort

Coastal lookout

a fuss and set about the construction of this fort. Never used as such, for a time it was the local prison, then was torn down and its stones hauled *mauka* to build Hale Pa'ahao, Lahaina's still-standing relic prison.

As its name implies, on the other side of Canal Street was once a canal, used as a landing by seamen coming to town from their ships on business. Adjacent to the canal was Rotten Row, more properly called Government Market, where commerce was conducted. The market burned down and the canal was filled in the early 1900s.

From Canal and Front streets, one can continue south on Front Street for a somewhat longer excursion, or else head directly up Prison Street. The longer excursion lacks visual splendor, but the history is interesting.

At the intersection of Front and Shaw streets is a faded little park, **Malu'ulu o Lele ❻**. It was once much more beautiful, evidently the residence for three of the Kamehameha kings, and before that, for the chiefs of Maui. There was a pond here, and in its center was a modest island, where there was not only the royal residence, but a royal tomb, its burial chamber decorated with mirrors, feather *kahili* marking royalty, luxurious velvet-covered chairs – and the coffins. After the monarchy collapsed, the tomb was removed and the pond covered over in 1918.

Continue *mauka* along Shaw Street to **Waiola Church ❼**, on Waine'e Street atop the site of Maui's first stone church, Waine'e Church, built in the early 1830s and able to seat 3,000 people on its dirt floor. For quite some time, this site lacked auspicious fortune. Between 1858 and 1951, the original church lost its roof and belfry to the wind, was burned down by Hawaiians angry at the overthrow of Queen Lili'uokalani, was rebuilt then damaged again by fire, rebuilt, and once more torn apart by winds. Rather than just await the next calamity, when the church was rebuilt again in 1953, it was also given a new name, Waiola, and it has has been okay ever since. Adjacent is Hawaii's first Christian cemetery, dating from the early 1820s. In addition to the missionary families and lonely seamen, Queen Ke'opuolani – one of Kamehameha the Great's wives and mother of both Kamehameha II and Kamehameha III – is buried here, a converted Protestant.

Head left, or north, on Waine'e Street, past the **Hongwanji Mission** (1927) to Prison Street, then left, where the high-walled ★ **Hale Pa'ahao ❽** stands in near-perfect condition, its massive stone walls surrounding a lush inner courtyard, in the middle of which is a wooden building with the prison cells. Translated as the 'stuck-in-iron house,' Hale Pa'ahao was built in the early 1850s during the reign of Kamehameha III, out of coral stone taken from the unused fort, near the Old Courthouse.

Queen Lili'uokalani

Hale Pa'ahao

While known for its casualness – picnics with visiting families in the central yard were common – the prison still had wall shackles and balls-in-chains for the truly criminal. Most prisoners, however, were stuck in iron for bad behavior, including 'furious' riding; disturbing the quiet of the night; drinking *awa* (a slightly narcotic drink found throughout the South Pacific); giving birth to bastard children; and affray. One 1850s prisoner, a 16-year-old seaman, wrote in his journal that 'no restrictions are placed on the use of cards or tobacco, and any sedate individual could therefore lay back all day with a pipe in his mouth and enjoy himself at a game of euchre as well as though he was comfortably stowed away in a beer house.'

Tropical tones

(If you've skipped the extended excursion and have come straight up Prison Street to this point, make sure that you first take a quick look in Dan's Greenhouse, on the left side of Prison Street, just half a block *mauka* from Front Street. You'll know you're there by the tropical birds singing away, and by the exquisite bonsai and orchids for sale inside.)

From Prison Street, walk north on **Luakini Street** towards the center of Lahaina. Luakini Street began as a path cleared through breadfruit and *koa* trees for the funeral procession of Princess Nahi'ena'ena in 1837. A Protestant who nonetheless wished to retain the old traditional ways, she had a son by her brother, Kamehameha III, a practice sometimes accepted in ancient Hawaii to retain the purity of the royal blood. The boy died shortly after birth, and she, four months later at the age of 21. (*Luakini* means a sacrificial *heiau*.)

25

Dwight Baldwin at his home, with part of the inventory

From Luakini, turn *makai* onto Dickenson Street. Where it meets Front Street, on the left is the ★ **Baldwin Home** ❾ (daily 10am–4.30pm), a two-story structure built of coral, stone and hand-cut timber. A Protestant medical missionary, Dwight Baldwin, made this his residence and clinic from the mid-1830s until the late 1860s, when he resettled in Honolulu. Baldwin came to Hawaii in 1835 to convert the inhabitants, but soon he was tending to Hawaiians taken ill by introduced Western diseases, including smallpox, which in the 1850s was nearly epidemic not only on Maui, but also on nearby Lanai and Molokai. The home also was a center of missionary activities on Maui, with a garden of both indigenous and introduced flora. Restored in the early 1960s, the house is now a museum, filled with antiques and furniture representative of the time. The Lahaina Restoration Foundation, which seeks to preserve historic buildings, has its offices here.

If visitors are going to walk along any single boulevard through Lahaina, it will necessarily be ★★ **Front Street**, which parallels the waterfront of Lahaina Harbor. Beyond

Cruising Front Street

About town

is **'Au'au Channel**, and Molokai and Lanai. (*'Au'au* means hurrying, or drenching; the channel is rough and exposed to the winds, and 'au'au suggests the state of people crossing its waters.) During the last ice age, the ocean was 300ft (100m) lower and Molokai and Lanai were part of a larger Maui, what geologists call Maui Nui, or Great Maui. The waters between the islands today are shallow and protected from the ocean's mood – perfect for the humpback whales that come down from Alaska in winter to breed and give birth.

The first whalers from New England came to Hawaii not for the humpbacks, but for the rest, replenishment and recreation available on the islands. Later, the whaling fleets stopped making annual journeys around the Cape and stayed in the Pacific year-round, using Hawaii as a base and depot for whale oil; merchant freighters would then make the trip back to New England with the oil.

Stop by **Ralston Antiques** (Monday to Saturday noon–9pm, Sunday 2–9pm), at Front Street and Lahainaluna Road, Hawaii's only real antique store and filled with what entrepreneur Rick Ralston couldn't fit in his own home or in the other establishments he has resuscitated. Founder of the Crazy Shirts chain found ubiquitously through Hawaii, Ralston has restored – and furnished with authentic period antiques – the Lahaina Inn, just up the street, and the Manoa Inn, in Honolulu. If there's something old and authentic in Hawaii, Ralston's hands are in there somewhere, polishing the patina.

Also on Front Street, Ralston's ★ **Lahaina Whaling Museum** (daily 9am–10pm) exhibits an excellent collection of whaling-period stuff that he has gathered over the years, both in Hawaii and in old New England whaling towns. Scrimshaw, an art form that originated out of the sailor's boredom while at sea, is especially interesting.

To pass the idle hours, seamen would carve delicate, intricate designs on whale teeth, then in later years on whalebone, walrus tusks and even wood. Much of the scrimshaw was clearly ornamental, yet at other times completely functional, including ivory clothespins. Also displayed are a valentine made of delicate shells – hundreds of them – and a figurehead from the original *Carthaginian*, carved twice its original size so as to be visible in the film *Hawaii*, in which the replacement brig was used.

Up half a block from Front Street on Lahainaluna Road is the **Lahaina Inn** ⓫, another of Ralston's restoration efforts. This richly restored 1860s-era hotel was first an inn for whalers and later for merchants. After a varied and checkered past, including a rebuilding, it was restored into what is now a real inn. The small lobby and a popular, Victorian-style bar and restaurant – David Paul's Lahaina Grill – occupy the ground floor, but on the second floor are 12 rooms of various sizes, all containing genuine antiques of the period. Rooms facing Lahainaluna Street and Front Street can be somewhat noisy, but their verandahs are good perches for people-watching and sunsets. Best for some, perhaps, is that no children under 15 are permitted. Further *mauka* on Lahainaluna is the **Plantation Inn**. Although of no historical interest, the inn is a congenial alternative to the standard resort or hotel, with less than two dozen rooms, an intimate ambiance, and the Pacific's best French restaurant, Gerard's.

Plantation Inn

Lahainaluna Road continues across the Honoapi'ilani Highway, Route 30, and past the **Pioneer Sugar Mill** ⓬, a Lahaina landmark for generations and one of the island's more successful sugar operations. At the top of Lahainaluna Road is **Lahainaluna High School**, dating from 1831 and earlier known as the Lahainaluna Seminary, established by Protestant missionaries. One of the original school buildings, **Hale Pa'i**, or the House of Printing (Monday to Friday 10am–2pm), is open as a museum. In this restored building is a replica of the original printing press carried from New England, which printed not only Hawaii's first newspaper – in Hawaiian and called *Ka Lama Hawaii* – but translations and textbooks. Lahainaluna High School itself was the first school in America west of the Rockies, established in the early 1830s as a missionary school. In the days of the Gold Rush in California, many Californians sent their children here for schooling, rather than risk the untamed overland trip east.

For a taste of sugar

Back on Front Street, most everyone walks the walk, tempted by schlock, schlock art, real art, and food. The places to eat are numerous, and few will fail you; while there are perennial stalwarts, however, some have lowered their standards as their notoriety with tourists has risen.

Collector's items

Two-story ★ **Wo Hing Society House** ⓭ is on the *mauka* side of Front Street and quickly identified by the Chinese characters above both gate and door, and a white picket fence. Although the Chinese population in Lahaina is exceedingly small, there was a time when the Chinese presence was considerable. (Probably the first Chinese were two businessmen who, in 1828, started a sugar mill on the island.) A member of a global Chinese fraternal society, Chee Kung Tong, which served as an extended family for the many single Chinese men, the Wo Hing Society House is an unpretentious and non-too-academic museum housing artifacts – an eleven-panel painted screen and jade *fu* dogs, for example – from the times of Chinese laborers and shopkeepers on Maui. The Wo Hing Society was founded in 1909 by Chinese cane-field laborers. The building dates from 1912, serving as a Wo Hing meeting hall until the 1940s, when it was turned into a residence for old men. To the right side is the cook shed, inside of which are not only old Chinese cooking utensils and fire pits, but screenings of old films made by Thomas Edison in Hawaii.

Wo Hing Society House

28

Most visitors go as far as the Lahaina Center, a successfully boring shopping center with a Hard Rock Cafe, but consider walking a little further. Just beyond the Hard Rock is the **Seamen's Hospital** ⓮, between Baker and Kenui streets. Currently not in use nor open to the public, it was restored and has an essential place in Lahaina's history. This dormant two-story building dates from the 1830s, built as a retreat for Kamehameha III and leased in 1844 to the American government as a hospital during Lahaina's whaling heydays. Sick or abandoned sailors, often with less-than-friendly social diseases, were cared for here. Then, in the mid-1860s, the building was sold for use as a Catholic school, later becoming a minister's vicarage. Abandoned in the early 1900s, it fell into decay until its restoration in the 1980s.

Amida Buddha at the Jodo Mission

Just beyond, near **Mala Wharf** at the north end of Lahaina, and across from the Lahaina Cannery, another shopping center, the **Jodo Mission Buddhist Cultural Park** ⓯ was built to commemorate the 100th anniversary, in 1968, of the arrival of Japanese plantation workers in Hawaii. Of interest is the large, 3½-ton **Amida Buddha** statue, said to be the largest of its kind outside Asia and facing the Maui sunset. Nearby are a pagoda and main temple, which has a classic bell, sounded by a long ramrod-like clapper hanging from chains. (Mala Wharf itself was built in the early 1920s as an alternative to Lahaina, but it proved unusable because of currents.)

One could follow Front Street back down to the center of town, so as to relive memories of the recent walk up Front Street, or else one could seek out a back street and explore.

Tour 3

Fertile Central Maui

Central Maui and the 'Iao Valley *See maps on pages 15 and 30–1*

29

Long ago, central Maui was nothing but water, a channel between a mature West Maui volcano and an adolescent Haleakala. The oceans retreated, lava from Haleakala filled in the gap, and a land bridge between the two volcanoes formed. It is Haleakala that gives the isthmus its undergirding, while erosion from West Maui has layered it with the rich soil that is important for agriculture today.

Central Maui is a crossover for travelers heading from the resorts of West Maui up Haleakala or around its northern flank to Hana. Geographically, the flat land of central Maui is undeniably static compared to the lush, deep valleys of West Maui and the sky-grabbing heights of Haleakala. For some dramatic contrast, this tour also takes in West Maui's 'Iao Valley, just a short drive from Wailuku.

Anchoring central Maui is the island's largest city and core of commerce, **Kahului**, flanked to the east by the airport and to the north by **Kahului Bay**. Captain Cook's ships, returning from a summer trip to Alaska, passed by the harbor but did not drop anchor. Nowadays, freighters and interisland cruise ships put in at **Kahului Harbor**, Maui's main deep-water port. Near the harbor is the **Maui Arts and Cultural Center**, off Kahului Beach Road and completed in 1995, a superb venue to performances of every persuasion. Kahului itself is a clutter of shopping malls and gas stations. Only locals intentionally go downtown, but if a standard American-style shopping mall is desperately required, the **Ka'ahumanu Shopping Center**, on Ka'ahumanu Avenue in central Kahului, will empty pockets in fine tradition.

Docking at Kahului Harbor

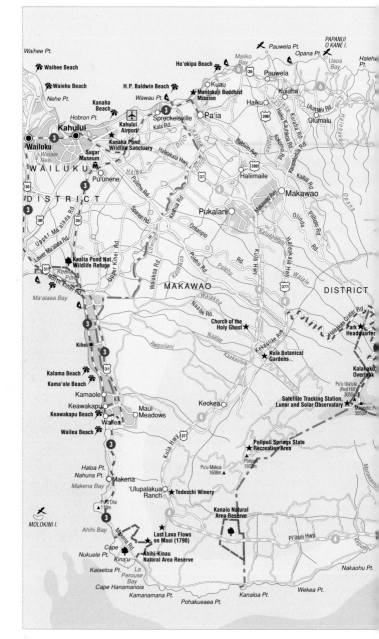

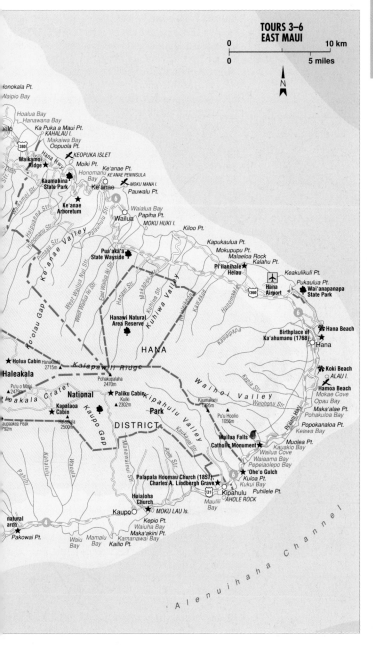

TOURS 3–6
EAST MAUI

0   10 km
0   5 miles

N

31

Honokala Pt.
Waipio Bay
Hoalua Bay
Hanawana Bay
elo
Ka Puka a Maui Pt.
KAHALAU I.
Makaiwa Bay
Oopuola Pt.
KEOPUKA ISLET
Waikamoi Ridge
Moiki Pt.
Ke'anae Pt.
Honomanu Bay
Ke'anae
Kaumahina State Park
Ke'anae KE'ANAE PENINSULA
MOKU MANA I.
Pauwalu Pt.
Ke'anae Arboretum
Waialua Bay
Papiha Pt.
Wailua
MOKU HUKI I.
Kiloo Pt.
Kapukaulua Pt.
Mokupupu Pt.
Malaeloa Rock
Pua'aka'a State Wayside
Kalahu Pt.
Pi'ilanihale Heiau
Keakulikuli Pt.
Pukaulua Pt.
Hana Airport
Wai'anapanapa State Park
Hanawi Natural Area Reserve
HANA
Birthplace of Ka'ahumanu (1768)
Hana Beach
Hana
Holua Cabin
Hanakauhi 2715m
Kalapawili Ridge
Koki Beach
ALAU I.
Haleakala
Pu'u o Maui 2479m
Pohakupalaha 2470m
National
Hamoa Beach
Mokae Cove
Opau Bay
Waihoi Valley
Maka'alae Pt.
Pohakuloa Bay
eakala Crater
Paliku Cabin
Kuiki 2302m
Kaumakani 1495m
Park
Kapalaoa Cabin
aupaakea Peak 792m
Haleakala 2500m
Pu'u Hoolio 1056m
Popokanaloa Pt.
Keawa Bay
Kaupo Gap
DISTRICT
Kipahulu Valley
Wailua Falls
Muolea Pt.
Catholic Monument
Kaukio Bay
Wailua Cove
Waiaama Bay
Pepeiaolepo Bay
Palapala Hoomau Church (1857), Charles A. Lindbergh Grave
'Ohe'o Gulch
Kuloa Pt.
Kukui Bay
Puhilele Pt.
Huialoha Church
10 MOKU LAU Is.
Kipahulu
AHOLE ROCK
natural arch
Kaupo
Kepio Pt.
Maka'akini Pt.
Maulili Bay
Pakowai Pt.
Waiu Bay
Mamalu Bay
Waihua Bay
Kamanawai Bay
Kailio Pt.

Alenuihaha Channel

Ka'ahumanu Church

Shades of the past in the Bailey House

On the periphery of all this urban clutter, and incongruously wedged between the airport and town, is the **Kanaha Pond State Wildlife Sanctuary**, said to have been built in the 16th century by a Maui chief. Despite the urban slop nearby, Kanaha Pond is not only a wintering stop for migratory birds such as shovelers and pintails from Alaska, but it is also home for the endangered Hawaiian stilt (*ae'o*) and Hawaiian coot (*'alae kea*). A lookout for bird-watching is accessed from the main highway between the airport and Kahului.

To the west of Kahului, *mauka* on Route 32 (Ka'ahumanu Highway) into the West Maui foothills, is the old town of ★ **Wailuku**, the seat of Maui County's government (which includes Lanai and Molokai). One of Hawaii's better preserved towns, it can make for an interesting couple of hours, with shops of quality junk to Thai restaurants of excellent fare, along with some authentic history.

New England-style **Ka'ahumanu Church**, at Main and High streets, was erected in 1876 of wood and stone to honor Kamehameha the Great's favorite wife, who after his death forced the collapse of the *kapu* system and the adoption of Christianity in the islands. Further *mauka* on Main Street a couple of hundred feet is ★★ **Hale Ho'ike-'ike** (daily 10am–4.30pm), a good example of early Western-style architecture in the islands, dating from the early 1830s and reflecting the melding of New England and Hawaii styles. Often called **Bailey House** and now a museum with an eclectic range of artifacts, both pre-contact and 19th century, the building is maintained by the Maui Historical Society. In 1842, Edward Bailey added what was then called the Wailuku Female Seminary, a boarding school for girls. The walls are made of coral blocks veneered in plaster; used for binder in the plaster was hair donated by the girls at the seminary.

In the same neighborhood, down the hill a bit, several government buildings are clustered together in Wailuku's central business district, along High Street and south of Main Street. Included in the National Register are Wailuku Courthouse (1907), County Office Building (1927), Wailuku Library (1928) and Territorial Building (1931). The last two structures were designed by noted Hawaiian architect C.W. Dickey. On the other side of Main Street, moored mostly along **Market Street**, are numerous older buildings that have been renovated, such as the 'Iao Theater and many restaurants and slightly eccentric, non-trendy shops.

Wailuku means waters of destruction, and it was up in the **West Maui Mountains**, in **'Iao Valley** and source of the water that flows into the ocean near Wailuku, that Kamehameha the Great fought his decisive battle over the defending chiefs of Maui. In the move to unify the islands under one ruler, Kamehameha had competition: Kahekili, of Maui. At the same time as Kamehameha was trying to subdue Maui, Kahekili was trying to conquer Oahu; he had left his son Kalanikupule in charge of Maui. With the help of black-powder weapons borrowed from Europeans, Kamehameha defeated Kalanikupule, thus effectively collapsing Kahekili's efforts. It was from 'Iao Valley that **'Iao Stream** flowed blood-red into the ocean near Wailuku, the stream clogged with the dead. After his defeat, Kalanikupule escaped by hiking over the ridge to the western coast, near Olowalu. Fate was against Kalanikupule, however; he finally fell to Kamehameha in the decisive battle of Nu'uanu Valley on Oahu, which effectively sealed Kamehameha's control over Hawaii.

The 'Iao Valley and its needle

Take Route 32, the main road through Kahului and Wailuku, straight up into the West Maui Mountains and 'Iao Valley. Once a sacred burial ground for chiefs and *ali'i*, 'Iao Valley (lit. cloud supreme) cuts right up to **Pu'u Kukui**, at 5,788ft (1,764m) the highest point in West Maui and one of the world's rainiest places – over 400 inches (10m) annually. (With so much rain falling on Pu'u Kukui, there is little moisture left in the trade winds when they reach Lahaina (lit. cruel sun), where it rarely rains. ★★ **'Iao Valley State Park** (daily 7am–7pm) is at the top of the road, at the base of 2,250-ft-high (685m) **'Iao Needle**, which rises 1,300ft (400m) above 'Iao Stream like a weather-tired, war-weary sentinel. In fact, it is an erosion-resistant dike from the West Maui volcano, with the delightful ancient Hawaiian name of Kukaemoku, or literally, broken excreta.

Kepaniwai colors

This is a resplendent and exquisite valley, well worth a couple of hours of wandering and daydreaming. There are some nice walking paths in the park, and fortunately, most of the people piling out of the tour buses never venture far from the parking lot. Spend some time here if you've got it. On the way out, at the valley's mouth and to the right of the road, is the **Kepaniwai Heritage Gardens**, a peace offering to the battles of the past, and a county park of gardens and pavilions reflecting the numerous groups – Hawaiian, Japanese, Chinese, Filipino and New Englander – that have settled on Maui.

From Wailuku, take Route 30 (High Street) south through Waikapu, where the **Hawaii Tropical Plantation** (daily 9am–5pm) lures packaged tours. There are some free and interesting agricultural exhibits, however, along with a pocket-emptying souvenir shop, and a not-so-free tram ride through fields of pineapple and orchards of papaya. Stop if you must, or if you want to see Hawaii's agriculture all together in a nice, neat package.

Route 30 shoots down towards the southern side of the central isthmus, which wraps around **Maʻalaea Bay**, usually smooth and, in winter, a good place to watch for the tell-tale spouting of whales (*see Tour 1, page 15*). Route 30 continues around the southern tip of West Maui and then up towards Lahaina, but, instead, take the Route 310 (N. Kihei Road) turnoff, towards Kihei and past the **Kealia Pond National Wildlife Refuge**. Access to the self-guided tour of this 500-acre (200 hectare) refuge, larger than Kanaha Pond, is on the ocean side, near North Kihei Road. This is the very last bit of honest nature before plunging into **Kihei**, a developed strip along the straight south-western coast, what some have condemned as condo-minium hell and what others call home, with six miles of non-stop shopping centers and condominiums. Yet some of the best deals in accommodations on Maui can be found here, especially for long-term stays, and the sun always shines on Kihei's decent beaches, including the creatively named **Kamaʻole I, II and III beaches**. Kihei gets trashed by both *kamaʻaina* and travelers, but for many people, Kihei makes a stay in Hawaii a reality. Just know that it's not especially idyllic, although at sunset, with one's back to the mess and one's eye on the horizon, it matters not.

If not keen on driving through Kihei's commercial wonders, take the Piʻilani Highway (Route 31) around Kihei, a high road that later drops down into ★ **Wailea**, in sharp contrast to Kihei. Wailea is the *aliʻi* stretch of this coast, a private development where there are only deluxe hotel resorts and equally deluxe condominiums and those ever-essential golfing venues. While some may say Wailea is rather sterile, its beautiful beaches are public, very nice, and blessed with splendid sunsets. In addition, hotels like the Four Seasons thoroughly seduce the most hardened skeptic. Next door to the Four Seasons is the Grand Wailea,

High-class Wailea

Wailea Beach

a half-billion-dollar, overbearing complex that sometimes borders on being goofy. But partly redeeming this property are the amusing ★ **Fernando Botero sculptures** of plump people and animals.

Wailea Alanui Road, Wailea's main thoroughfare, continues south along golf courses towards drier **Makena**. (More accurately, actually, is that Wailea is artificially greener.) There's but one hotel here, the Maui Prince, pleasantly isolated at the south end of the coast; the Prince's marbled everything takes the edge off the rustic *kiawe* surroundings. Beyond the Maui Prince, on a small spur road looping along Makena Bay, **Keawala'i Church**, made of coral blocks and one of Maui's earliest churches, sits looking out over the water.

The road continues further south another couple of miles, almost all the way to **Cape Kina'u**, formed when Maui's last volcanic eruption, in 1790, sent floods of lava into the ocean from a rift fracture on the lower slopes directly above us and below 'Ulupalakua Ranch and Tedeschi Winery (*see Tour 4, page 40*). Looking at a map, one would expect a convenient road between Makena and Upcountry. There is, but it's for four-wheel-drive vehicles, and it's very private, with a locked gate. To reach Upcountry, it's necessary to drive back to central Maui and Kahului.

The road effectively ends just before Cape Kina'u, but if it were to continue further along the coast, it would follow the ancient route of the **Hoapili**, or the King's Trail, the path of royal travel that once nearly encircled the island (*see also Tour 4, page 41*). It's possible to take a four-wheel-drive vehicle along the southern coast. Otherwise, if wishing to see something ancient like this, go to the Big Island, where, near the Mauna Lani Bay Hotel, there is a King's Trail that is well worn into the lava and passing through superb fields of petroglyphs – and all within a five-minute walk from the car (and from a golf course).

About 7 miles (11km) off Wailea is **Kaho'olawe**, an uninhabited and mostly flat island, the smallest of Hawaii's eight main islands and about 45 sq miles (115 sq km) in area. The island is scattered with ancient historic sites, many of them on the National Register of Historic Places. As its soil is poor – it sits in Haleakala's rain shadow, Kaho'olawe was probably used as a home away from home by Hawaiian fishermen. More recently, in the 19th century, smugglers used the island as a handy place to cache shipments of opium.

The US Navy was given complete jurisdiction over the island in the early 1950s, using it as a gunnery range for the next four decades. (Fortunately, the archeological sites were off limits to the guns.) This target practice

Botero sculpture in the Grand Wailea

Happy hour at Makena

Sunset at Cape Kin'au

Molokini

*Alexander & Baldwin: tools
of the trade*

kindled the resolve of Native Hawaiian activists, who fought for the return of Kahoʻolawe to Hawaii's control in the late 1960s and early 1970s. Eventually a compromise was reached in the mid-1970s, permitting Native Hawaiians to go ashore at times to tend to sacred matters. The island has now been returned to the state, no longer targeted by the Navy, but scores of unexploded armaments remain, making portions of the island lethal.

The channel between Kahoʻolawe and nearby Lanai is **Kealaikahiki**, meaning the way to foreign lands, but, more specifically, the way to Tahiti. It was through this channel that ancient ocean-going canoes probably made their way between Maui and the South Pacific.

Crystal-clear offshore between Maui and Kahoʻolawe rises the 80-ft-high (25m) crescent tuff cone of **Molokini**, a seabird sanctuary and marine conservation area. It is also one of the Pacific's most in-demand snorkeling sites, confirmed by the numerous boats that are anchored there every morning. A tuff cone like Oahu's Diamond Head, Molokini was formed when rising magma hit a pocket of water below ground; the superheated water turned to steam, forcing up an explosion of rock, ash and steam.

Reverse directions and drive back through Wailea and downtown Kihei, or else take the Piʻilani Highway around Kihei. At the top end of Kihei, Route 35, the Mokulele Highway, shunts around the eastern side of Kealia Pond and straight north through expanses of sugar cane that cover central Maui. The road comes to an abrupt left turn in **Puʻunene**, confronted by its operating sugar mill dating from the early 1900s. This working town exists only for sugar. Past the mill – follow the signs – is the ★ **Alexander & Baldwin Sugar Museum**, which should be visited, even if briefly. In this former plantation manager's home built in 1902, there are excellent exhibits not only about sugar and its processing but also about Maui's traditional plantation life, and the lifestyles of Hawaii's early immigrants who came to work in the fields.

From Puʻunene, one could return to Kahului, or else join the Hana Highway or Haleakala Highway eastward. A pleasant, short round-trip drive is to take the Haleakala Highway, Route 37, up towards Pukalani and Makawao, then come back down Route 390 and rejoin the Hana Highway at Paʻia.

At the start of the **Hana Highway**, just east of the airport, is the phantom town of Spreckelsville, named after Claus Spreckels, a sugar baron, and a place that seems to exist in a spatial if not perceptual vacuum. Further on and much easier to find is the old sugar town of ★ **Paʻia**, now the proverbial funky alternative-lifestyle windsurfing town, increasingly tourist savvy. Several 'funky' eater-

ies – offering hearty breakfasts and lunches – and nearly an equal number of 'funky' shops are worth a stop. At the signal in downtown Pa'ia, the road leading up towards Haleakala goes through **Makawao** (*see Tour 4, page 38*).

Blue skies over Pa'ia

Less than half a mile past Pa'ia's signal and fronting the ocean is the **Mantokuji Buddhist Mission**, reflecting the influence of Japanese immigrants and typical of such architecture in Hawaii. This mission is from the early 1920s, and the adjacent cemetery has over 600 burial markers, some in English but mostly in Japanese; if here in late summer, join in the Obon festivities, a Japanese time for honoring the ancestral ghosts.

Beyond, the Hana Highway takes on more rustic contours. Keep an eye out for ★★ **Ho'okipa Beach**, justifiably the world-class windsurfing center of the explored universe. Years back, when it was discovered that the waters just off this beach consistently churn up perfect conditions for windsurfing, the fading sugar town of Pa'ia regained its dignity with a new kind immigrant, albeit often itinerant and questionably solvent. Just to the east of Ho'okipa is a bluff with a parking lot, a perfect place to watch the windsurfers rip through the waves in intentionally choreographed somersaults and flips. Many of those itinerant windsurfers are now professionals, some earning six-figure incomes through competition and endorsements.

Windsurfing at Ho'okipa

Continuing east, the Hana Highway slices inland a bit, rises and drops for a few miles before beginning its twisting way to Hana. There are several stops along the Hana Highway that one might consider taking in on this itinerary, without going all the way to Hana (*see Tour 6, page 50*). Or, if choosing to go Upcountry (*see Tour 4*), do so by taking little-used Route 365, through **Ulumalu**. Or just hang out at Ho'okipa, frustrated that you chose the wrong lifestyle.

Tour 4

Upcountry's mist-shrouded forests

In driving mileage, there's not much to Upcountry proper, perhaps 30 miles (50km) of road altogether. But Upcountry is one of Maui's more popular places to live, where one can cozy up to a fireplace or take in an early morning's tangy air. Scents of eucalyptus sift through these highlands, while mists linger lazily on the higher slopes. Visitors find Upcountry an unexpected treat – wine, flowers, coffee, mist-shrouded forests – yet the ocean and beaches are always in view, and accessible in a fast retreat.

Upcountry is a temperate zone on Haleakala's northwestern slope, at about 3,000ft (900m) in elevation and extending from Pukalani and Makawao down to Haleakala's southwest rift, where the island's last volcanic activity happened two centuries ago. One can extend Upcountry travels – highly recommended for a primal view of Maui – and continue past this rift to Maui's south coast towards Kaupo, skirting Haleakala's southern side. Unless coming this way – in reverse – around Maui's southern coast by way of Hana and Kipahulu, a rather long route if not spending a night or more in Hana, the only way to Upcountry is from the north, through Makawao and Pukalani. Logic and a map argue for access from Makena and Wailea (*see Tour 3, pages 34–5*), but save for a private four-wheel-drive track, there is nothing.

Taking the high road

The **Haleakala Highway** starts at the Kahului Airport and rises to **Pukalani**, which means heavenly gate. When the prevailing northeastern trade winds are deflected around Haleakala's slopes over central Maui, the clouds that form as the wet air is pushed upwards tend to swirl and break open right above Pukalani, a metaphorical gate to the heights of Haleakala. Other than a golf course, Pukalani has done little to entice tourists, unlike its neighbor, ★ **Makawao**. Makawao has remade itself in the image that

Makawao local

upscale professionals living in the area and tourists from afar like. Upcountry is ranch land, and Makawao (lit. forest beginning) straddled the sugar plantations lower down and the ranches of Upcountry. Quite frankly, the hype about Makawao nowadays is overdone, as the *paniolo* town image it tries to maintain has been eclipsed, except during the Fourth of July Makawao Rodeo, by boutiques and restaurants. (Excellent ones, by the way.)

The Haleakala Highway passes directly between Pukalani and Makawao, continuing up country; a minute beyond, entering the **Kula** district, a turnoff takes the Haleakala Highway away from the main road to become a high road. The lower road becomes the Kula Highway.

All along both highways are flower farms and gardens, selling brilliant heliconias, birds of paradise, orchids – and the Protea, an unusual tropical flower related to, obscurely enough, the macadamia, but of much grander and more resplendent appearance. When dried, the large Proteas can be shipped anywhere as gifts.

The resplendent Protea

The Kula area is probably Hawaii's most diversified agricultural area, albeit on a small scale, growing everything from sweet onions to apples and pears, not to forget lettuce, cabbage and peas, and lately, coffee. A lot of this produce ends up in Hawaii's finer restaurants. Just before the road to Haleakala, on the right, is the **Kula Lodge**, a decent place for lunch, with a few cottages for rent. Other than some bed-and-breakfast places further on, this is all there is for accommodation in Upcountry.

Six miles after leaving the main road, the Haleakala Highway once again breaks away from the road, at the turnoff for **Haleakala National Park**. From here, Haleakala Crater Road takes its time ascending numerous switchbacks – over 30 – up Haleakala's slopes towards the summit. If ascending in mid-morning, watch out for the bicycle caravans coming down the mountain, propelled by gravity and a sense of immortal empowerment.

39

Three miles beyond the Haleakala turnoff, the high road descends back down to the main road, still called the Kula Highway. A small park and lookout at the junction is a good place to let the kids vent steam. Had we taken the low road, Kula Highway, through Upcountry, rather than the Haleakala high road, we would have passed an unusual, octagonal-shaped building on the right side of the road: the **Church of the Holy Ghost**, erected in 1894 by Portuguese immigrants who arrived in Hawaii a generation earlier as sugar plantation laborers. It was renovated in the early 1990s. Inside is a beautiful hand-carved altar.

Church of the Holy Ghost

Preserving the local vernacular

Grandma's Coffee House

Tedeschi wines and winery

The highway weaves southward through pasture land, reaching Upcountry's last significant residential area of **Keokea**, with a store, gas station and Grandma's, a restaurant offering good food and fortified desserts, and a selection of Maui-grown coffee. As with coffee from the Big Island's Kona district, know that if buying a blend, you are getting only 10 percent of the local bean; the rest can be from anywhere, like New Jersey. Make sure you get the 100 percent stuff.

The Kula Highway becomes quite narrow and roller-coaster like past Keokea, and quite a delight to drive. When the light is low and just right, the colors of the pasture land and trees take on a magical hue, more what one might expect to experience in Scotland or Kentucky than in Hawaii. In spring, the whole area is filled with brilliant purple blossoms. The road has several blind crests and curves, so take extra care.

Trees start seriously gathering just before the road enters **'Ulupalakua**, headquarters for the 20,000-acre (8,000 hectares) 'Ulupalakua Ranch, a working outfit with around 5,000 head of cattle, along with some sheep and elk. 'Ulupalakua (lit. breadfruit ripening on the backs of carriers) started out as a sugar plantation, and out in the bush somewhere is what remains of an 1878 sugar mill.

At the other end of 'Ulupalakua, on the left, is the ★ **Tedeschi Winery** (daily 9am–5pm). Those travelers who have made the wine-tasting circuits of California's Napa Valley or Australia's Victoria region, not to mention those of France, might choose to smirk and continue on, or turn around and go back to the hotel. But where else might one try a sweet but decent pineapple wine? There's not just pineapple wine to be sipped here, too; a champagne and some red and white wines are also offered. Started by a vintner from Napa in the mid-1970s, the winery's small visitors center and wine-tasting room was once a jail; the winery is compact, but do take the tour if not familiar with wine-making. The microclimate in this part of Upcountry (cool and dry) is nearly perfect for the 20 acres (8 hectares) of Carnelian grapes that grow in the volcanic soil.

Car rental companies might have you believe that the road ends here by dropping off the earth, threatening in rental contracts the worst of fire and brimstone should you continue onwards. But Maui's most remote and primal setting, other than Haleakala's summit, is further on. Just past the winery, the road bends due east, changing its name from the Kula Highway to the **Pi'ilani Highway**, and crossing Haleakala's southeastern rift. Just below the bend in the road is the site of Haleakala's – and Maui's – last volcanic activity, around 1790. Lava flows from two vents, one at 1,500ft (460m) above sea level and the other at 570ft (175m), joined in a single flow that was 3 miles (5km) wide when it hit the ocean in a swoosh of steam and exploding lava. While no Westerner was around to actually witness the eruption, the evidence is rather solid: La Pérouse mapped a shallow bay here in 1786, while Vancouver found a large peninsula of fresh lava in the same spot five years later, now called **Cape Kina'u** and designated a nature reserve.

Pi'ilani Highway

41

On the south side of Cape Kina'u is **La Pérouse Bay**, formed by the 1790 flow and named after the Frenchman who was the first European to set foot on Maui, in 1786. (Captain Cook merely sailed past Maui, although he did note the presence of Haleakala – *see page 43*). La Pérouse wrote of 'four small villages of about ten or twelve houses each, built and covered with straw…', and where he traded for provisions. He then sailed his two ships to the northwest along the Hawaiian chain, where the expedition was nearly shipwrecked on the shoal named, following his visit, French Frigate Shoal. La Pérouse then left the Hawaiian islands and disappeared forever.

The change in climate and scenery is marked here. Empty as it might appear now, the area on Haleakala's south flank, east of Kina'u, was substantially populated in pre-contact times. The rugged coastline is peppered with ancient Hawaiian structures, from canoe sheds to *heiau*.

Heiau temple east of Kina'u

Inaccessible to rental cars is **Hoapili**, or the King's Trail, an extensive footpath that once encircled most of Maui (*see also Tour 3, page 35*). Today, parts of the trail remain along the coast east of Kina'u, with some additional sections north of Hana (*see Tour 6, page 53*). The 2- to 3-meter-wide trail, constructed of fitted boulders and blocks of lava that leveled the walk across the inhospitable terrain of the area, was used by chiefs and *ali'i*, or royalty.

From 'Ulupalakua to Hana on the Pi'ilani Highway is 37 miles (60km), all but five miles of which is surfaced with passable asphalt. Scores of rental cars and a few tour minibuses make the trip daily, unless it's been raining, which makes the 5 miles (8km) of washboard gravel road a bit awkward and perhaps impassable in a sub-compact automobile.

Whale-watching from the highway

The Pi'ilani Highway makes a straight and gradual descent eastward from the rift zone down to the ocean, passing over relatively new land covered with only grass and *kiawe* bushes, and cattle roaming on the open range. Foundations of old homesteads are scattered in the grass. Up on Haleakala's slope, at about 3,000ft (900m) above the harsh coastline, there was once a major Hawaiian settlement, Kahiki Nui, whose inhabitants constructed a sophisticated water containment system. Heavily populated at the time of Cook's arrival in Hawaii, the settlement was spread out over extensive step terraces. Kahiki Nui's name takes on a ghostly, ancient significance when translated: Great Tahiti.

Frangipani

42

The road touches the coast at Huakini Bay, where the basaltic cliffs harbor a natural arch. Near here was the village of Nu'u, where Hawaiians carved depressions in the stone, filled them with salt water, and let the sun extract the salt. The summit of Haleakala rises 7 miles (11km) to the north. At the eastern end of the bay is where massive lava flows came pouring down from Haleakala's basin through the **Kaupo Gap**, one of the two primary breeches in the basin's rim. The road passes right over this flow from Kaupo Gap, losing its asphalt midway across. **St Joseph Church**, on the right and built in 1861, announces the hamlet of ★ **Kaupo**, increasingly reshaping itself for the modest tourist trade bouncing and rattling past (check out the general store), and endowed with a cryptic meaning – landing place of canoes at night. Up slope on the Kaupo Gap lava flow are numerous *heiau* from the 16th century; a trail leads up through the Kaupo Gap to join the national park's trail system at Paliku Cabin, in Haleakala's summit basin.

Kaupo sunset

Half a mile past Kaupo is perhaps the most picturesque setting for a church in Hawaii, where **Huialoha Church**, dating from 1859, is eternally windswept, but still used just enough to keep it from blowing away. Offshore are the numerous rocky islets known as Moku Lau.

From Kaupo, it is 6 miles (10km) to **Kipahulu**. Along the way, the road hugs the coast in a set of sharp hills and equally sharp turns before pavement returns. If the road is wet, and especially if rains have been recent, think twice before continuing. Or wait for a car coming from Hana, and ask about the road.

Tour 5

Haleakala *See map on page 44*

Were it possible to gouge from the earth the island of Manhattan, with or without its hordes of yellow taxis, but with all of its skyscrapers, it would fit into the basin crater atop Haleakala. Easily. Not only would it fit in length and breadth, but skyscrapers like the twin towers of the World Trade Center would sink humbly below the rim of Haleakala.

Beholding the sublime

The summit of Haleakala is deceptive to behold, for there are no familiar visual references for scale or depth. Even its overall appearance from afar – like all Hawaiian islands, that of a shield volcano – is illusory. Captain James Cook didn't stop on Maui, but sailed past on his way to the Big Island from Alaska, noting conservatively, even for an Englishman, that Haleakala was 'an elevated hill... whose summit rose above the clouds.' Had he stopped and ascended Haleakala, he might have preempted the words from Mark Twain, who wrote of a summit sunrise atop Haleakala: 'It was the sublimest spectacle I ever witnessed, and I think the memory of it will remain with me always.' For Twain, those too were reserved words, so unlike him. Words do often fail when confronted with the awesome.

43

Haleakala is one of two volcanoes making up Maui. West Maui, the other, is the older of the two. Haleakala's prime period of volcanic activity was around 1 million years ago. It last erupted around 1790, not up at the top, as one might expect, but rather on its lower flanks, much as Kilauea now erupts on the Big Island's lower extents. Haleakala is more triangular than round, with each side about 25 miles

Haleakala's gigantic crater

A popular means of descent

The clouds billow at sunrise

(40km) in length. It is one of the planet's most massive mountains, with just 7 percent of it above water, and the remainder rising 5 miles (8km) from its base on the ocean floor. (In fact, the volcanic cones that make up the Hawaiian islands are the earth's most massive individual structures, save for continents. The mass of the Hawaiian islands is so great that they actually bend the earth's crust far below at about one inch per decade.)

Haleakala is tall enough above water, however, that it rises above the level of clouds formed by the prevailing trade winds. The result is that, while the slopes on the windward side, which includes Hana, are exceedingly wet and lush, the summit is dry and desiccated. Nevertheless, given its mass, Haleakala pulls 9 million tons of water from the clouds *daily* as rain; four percent of this fills the streams gushing down its slopes, the rest sinking below ground to the water table.

There was a time, long before Captain Cook or Mark Twain, when the sun liked to sleep late, then make up lost time by double-timing across the big sky. Hina, mother of the demigod Maui, could not dry her *tapa* cloth during the short day. A good if not impish son, Maui hid one night in a cave near the top of Haleakala, bringing with him over a dozen snare ropes of *'ie'ie*, a strong vine that grows in Hana. As the sunrise sliced across Haleakala's lofty top, Maui snagged the shafts of sunlight with his ropes, and held on to the sun until it agreed to move across the sky more slowly.

The sunrise atop Haleakala (lit. house of the sun) is exquisite, but so too is the sunset, when far fewer people crowd around you, and there's no need to arise at 3am to make the one- to two-hour drive to the summit. Far more relaxing is watching the sun settle *into* the ocean from Haleakala, then descending hotel-ward for a starlit dinner.

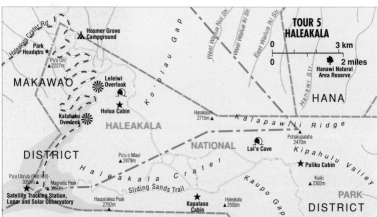

TOUR 5 HALEAKALA

Hosmer Grove Campground

Park Headqtrs

Haleakala Crater Rd.

Pu'u Oili ▲2227m

MAKAWAO

Leleiwi Overlook

Ko'olau Gap

West Wailua Nui Str.

West Wailua Iki Str.

East Wailua Iki Str.

Hanawi Str.

0 — 3 km
0 — 2 miles

Hanawi Natural Area Reserve

HANA

Holua Cabin

Kalahaku Overlook

HALEAKALA

Hanakauhi 2715m▲

Kalapawili Ridge

DISTRICT

Pu'u o Maui ▲2479m

NATIONAL

Lai'e Cave

Pohakupalaha 2470m

Kipahulu Valley

Pu'u Ula'ula (Red Hill) 3055m▲

Magnetic Peak ▲3060m

Satellite Tracking Station, Lunar and Solar Observatory

Haleakala Crater

Sliding Sands Trail

Haupa'akea Peak 2792m▲

★ Paliku Cabin

Kaupo Gap

Kuiki ▲2302m

Kapalaoa Cabin

Haleakala ▲2500m

PARK DISTRICT

An ascent of Haleakala begins at the Upcountry turnoff from Highway 377, the **Haleakala Highway**, the high road through the Kula district, onto Route 378, passing orchid and protea farms and easing through groves of eucalyptus and across grassy pastures, winding and twisting upwards towards the summit on over 30 switchbacks. Before long, it's actually chilly, with a mist oozing across the slopes. In fact, the temperature has been dropping about 3° F with every 1,000ft (300m) in elevation gain. (In winter, for road conditions on the top, tel: 572 7749.)

The snaking Haleakala Highway

The view is increasingly spectacular. On the other side of the isthmus is West Maui, the island's older volcano that rose before Haleakala. By the time the road reaches the summit in just under 40 miles (65km), the road has come from sea level to over 10,000ft (3,000m); those who calculate these interesting things claim Haleakala is the only place in the world where any road does such. It matters not, really, but what does is that gas and food need to be purchased at Pukalani or Makawao, if not before. There are neither gas stations nor stores anywhere on the mountain or in the national park.

45

At around 6,700ft (2,000m) in elevation, ★★★ **Haleakala National Park** begins; the main visitor center at the end of the road is about 11 miles (18km) further. Haleakala National Park protects 27,000 acres (67,000 hectares) of Haleakala's summit, rain forest and endangered ecosystem. Created in 1916 as part of Hawaii Volcanoes National Park, Haleakala broke off from its Big Island mate in 1961 to become Hawaii's second national park. Additional areas were later added to the park, including Kipahulu Valley – so fragile as one of Hawaii's last refuges of indigenous species of plants and birds that it is closed to the public – and a small slice of the Hana Coast at the base of Kipahulu Valley. In 1981, the park was designated an International Biosphere Reserve by the United Nations.

Zooming in on the view

One-half mile beyond the park boundary is **Hosmer Grove**, a campground with picnic tables, fireplaces, toilets and drinking water. No permit is required to camp here, but only 3 nights total each month are allowed. The site is named after the Territory of Hawaii's first forester, who in 1910 planted eucalyptus, spruce and pine trees here in an effort to revive Maui's watershed, and to grow fuel for the island's sugar mills. An easy half-mile-long trail passes through, first, groves of the introduced species of flora, then through indigenous shrubland. Bird watchers will see both native and introduced species along the way.

Another half mile further is the ★ **park headquarters** and a visitors center, with facilities, (daily 7.30am–4pm). Elevation is nearly 7,000ft (2,100m) and the air can feel uncomfortably chilly. This is also about as high as clouds dare go. In addition to exhibits, the visitors center has a modest selection of books and maps, and information about back-country permits and trail conditions.

Unique to Hawaii: the nene

If not planning to hike or take a short walk, then the park headquarters is perhaps the best chance to see the *nene,* or Hawaiian goose, unique to Hawaii. The nene was once common to Haleakala, numbering in the tens of thousands. Hunting – along with the introduction of the mongoose (intended to control rats, unsuccessfully, but successful in eliminating 75 percent of Hawaii's native birds by eating their eggs) – nearly made the nene extinct. In the early 1950s, there were less than three dozen nene in all of Hawaii, all of them on the Big Island and half of them in captivity. The nene has made a modest, although still-precarious comeback, with reintroduced populations at Hawaii Volcanoes National Park, on the Big Island, here on Haleakala, and on Kauai. It is punishable by fine and federal jail time to harass or disturb the nene, and *that includes feeding them.*

Pahoehoe's gnarled forms

A'a is abrasive on the shoes

Although possibly related, distantly, to Canada geese, the nene has evolved into a new species. The nene is a high-altitude fowl, having no use for ponds and lakes, and thus no use for webbed feet. It's a good thing the nene lacks webbing, for it must negotiate difficult terrain of lava. There are two types of lava common in Hawaii: *a'a* (ah-ah) and *pahoehoe* (pa-hoy-hoy), both Hawaiian words that have been adopted by geologists around the world. Pahoehoe is smooth and sensuously convoluted, its plastic crust having been dragged and wrinkled by underlying liquid lava into tapestry-like folds and rolls resembling twisted rope. Created by faster-flowing lava streams, a'a, on the other hand, is distinguished by its eat-up-the-shoes texture: rugged, jagged and extremely abrasive. Much of the lava on the slopes where the nene waddle is a'a.

Coming up or going down, stop at **Leleiwi Overlook**, 8,800ft (2,700m) in elevation and atop a *pali* at the summit basin's west end. With the sun overhead in late afternoon, and if clouds have lingered in the basin below, your shadow may be cast upon the clouds to create the 'specter of Brocken' effect, with a halo surrounding your shadow on the clouds. (This is often seen from airplanes flying above clouds, too.) Hawaiians called the phenomenon *ho'okuaka.* On the ground, it is seen in only three places in the world, one of which is Haleakala.

Descending into the basin

Haleakala's basin is 7½ miles (12km) long, 2½ miles (4km) wide, and 21 miles (35km) in circumference, but it doesn't seem so large at first look. One of the larger cones in the basin, **Pu'u o Maui**, is 1,000ft (300m) high from its base, but it's nearly lost down there. The basin is often mistakenly referred to as a crater or caldera, but both terms are geologically incorrect. In fact, Haleakala's concave basin was created by wind and water erosion. About 100,000 years ago, the rain lashing Haleakala was considerably more than nowadays, and two deep valleys, Ke'anae and Kaupo, eroded so much that they joined at their tops to form the giant basin. During this period of intensive erosion, almost 4,000ft (1,200m) of mountain was removed from Haleakala's original height. The summit basin, too, was once deeper, but subsequent volcanic activity – note the many cinder cones that mark the basin, with as many as 2,500 small eruptions over the past several thousand years – buried much of the basin.

A mile further is the ★★ **Kalahaku Overlook**, 9,000ft (2,700m) above sea level, with much of the same view as Leleiwi, but maybe better. To the left (north), where the *pali* melt away, is the gap leading to Ke'anae Valley; directly ahead on the other side of the basin and out of sight is Kipahulu Valley, which descends to Hana; and off to the right is the obvious Kaupo Gap, spilling out down the southern slopes to the ocean. There is a modest exhibit explaining Haleakala's geology, and, of course, it overlooks Haleakala's immense basin. If here in the summer, especially July or August, be sure to look for the silverswords, or *'ahinahina,* one of the world's rarest plants and found near the overlook in a protected enclosure. *'Ahinahina* means grey-grey in Hawaiian. A relative of the sunflower that reaches 3 to 8 feet in height, the silversword grows for 5 to 20 years, blooms once in its last summer with several hundred small, yellow or purplish flowers, then dies. The plant looks odd, almost industrial, but is perfectly designed for its high-altitude habitat. A 19th-century traveler atop Haleakala wrote that she came upon 'thousands of silverswords, their cold, frosted gleam making the hillside look like winter or moonlight.' When the park was established in 1916, the plant was virtually extinct. Not

Kalahaku Overlook

Silverswords

Visitors Center at sunrise

Sliding Sands Trail

Visitors on Red Hill

only did tourists of the time yank up the plants and roll them down the slopes, apparently to great affect, but the introduced feral and domesticated stock that roamed Haleakala devastated their delicate ecosystem. (In fact, until the 1920s, the huge Haleakala Ranch, which still exists back down the mountain, encompassed the summit; cattle were herded up over the rim and into the basin.) Although now protected by both law and fencing around the park, the silversword is still threatened with extinction by the introduced Argentine ant, which preys on the silversword's prime pollinators.

Haleakala Visitors Center (daily, sunrise to 3pm), 11 miles (18km) from the park boundary, is a warm respite from the often chilly winds. During the summer, there are ranger-guided nature walks – nothing too strenuous – lasting from 30 minutes to a couple of hours. The trail head for the popular ★ **Sliding Sands Trail** starts near here. Sliding Sands, more lyrically known in Hawaiian as **Keonehe'ehe'a**, and with the same meaning, provides a good introduction to Haleakala. Indeed, it's well worth walking it even if just for a hundred yards, for not until one has descended into the basin is Haleakala's sheer vastness embraced so completely.

The heights of Haleakala did not deter Hawaiians from climbing it. In fact, rather than crossing the island by going around Haleakala – pushing through low-altitude rain forests and deep valleys – they came directly over the top of Haleakala along a major footpath that crossed the summit basin. In 1922, a researcher mapped the trail, including its marker stones, and the numerous altars, terraced platforms and stone enclosures along its route; drifting sands have subsequently covered most of them, and the trail.

★★ **Pu'u Ula'ula**, less than a mile beyond the visitors center and Haleakala's highest point at 10,023ft (3,055m), is also known as **Red Hill**, the English translation. A glass-enclosed overlook with 360-degree views is popular with those up here for the sunrise, when the air is frigid. The original summit of Haleakala, perhaps 4,000ft (1,200m) higher, was about a mile east of Pu'u Ula'ula. A few yards to the southeast and 15ft lower is Magnetic Peak, named for the geophysical weirdness it induces into compasses.

Just before the road to Pu'u Ula'ula ends at the parking lot, a spur road cuts off towards **Kolekole**, a perceptible 10ft lower than Pu'u Ula'ula, outside of the national park, and closed to the public. Kolekole is topped by a cluster of sinister-looking domes, and is called by the occasional poet Science City, with numerous academic and

Kolekole's 'Science City'

government research facilities, including a solar and lunar observatory run by the University of Hawaii, and a Department of Defense satellite tracking station.

Not so long ago, a brilliant green laser light left here for the moon, to be reflected back to Haleakala by a small (1 sq m) reflector left on the moon by an Apollo mission. Not only was the distance to the moon calculated to within centimeters, but plate tectonics and continental drift was accurately measured, and it was confirmed that Maui, like all the Hawaiian islands, was moving to the northwest.

Camping at Haleakala

Trails lace the basin on Haleakala's summit. As elsewhere in the national park system, the National Park Service requires a back-country permit for overnight stays in the Haleakala wilderness. Unlike most other national parks, however, the ecosystem of Haleakala is especially unique, and especially threatened by the mildest of abuse. Don't flaunt the rules. Stay on trails; that small green plant you step upon in your wanderlust may be the last of its species on the planet.

Tread carefully

Back-country permits for using one of the three overnight cabins on Haleakala are free and issued on a first-come, first-serve basis. Applications must be received 3 months prior to one's planned visit; write to Superintendent, Haleakala National Park, P.O. Box 369, Makawao 96768. Provide alternative dates; the sites are popular.

The rustic cabins hold up to 12 people, and have a wood-burning stove, cooking utensils, bunks and firewood. Chemical toilets are nearby, and water is brought in by the park service, although it must be purified. Dates are chosen by lottery, and a fee of $40 per night is charged for 1 to 6 people, and $80 per night for 7–12. Only one group is permitted to use the cabin, regardless of the number of people in the group.

49

Along the Hana Coast

Tour 6

Hana Coast *See map on pages 30–1*

Destination the beach

Before buying into the T-shirt hype and thinking that a visit to Hana is a journey of monumental undertaking, understand that driving the road to Hana is not a feat of endurance, much less one of survival. Driving the Santa Monica Freeway is, as is driving crosstown in Manhattan. The road to Hana, on the other hand, is pure pleasure. It's just slow, that's all.

Along the 55 miles (90km) between Kahului and Hana, those with no creative life have counted over 600 curves and over 50 bridges along the ★★ **Hana Highway**. (The multitudinous waterfalls, however, still need counting.) Yes, the Hana Highway is a narrow and winding road, with bottlenecks of rubber-necking rental cars all trying to get to Hana by mid-morning. Free-thinkers should consider staying a night in Hana – after 5pm, the roads and pools and ocean are virtually all yours, until around mid-morning the following day.

At the end of this nefariously beautiful road is, of course, the town of Hana, with but 2,500 people in the greater Hana metropolitan area, and beyond, the 'Ohe'o pools and Kipahulu Valley, part of Haleakala National Park. The road doesn't actually end, however. Despite rental-car company frenzied concerns, it's actually possible to continue driving past Kipahulu around the southern end of Maui and back Upcountry, completely circling around Haleakala.

The Hana Highway itself was first opened in the 1920s, sculpted out of difficult terrain using convict labor. Forty years later, it was finally paved, and in 1984, overhauled once again. Considering that around half a million people travel over it yearly, it remains in good condition.

Regardless of where you start on Maui, eventually all roads converge at the northern shore, on Route 36/360. Stop for breakfast and pick-up picnic lunches in **Pa'ia** (*see Tour 3, page 36*) then follow the signs eastward towards Hana. There are several scenic stops during the first few miles towards Hana; dither too long, however, and you'll find yourself spending but 10 minutes in Hana before turning around to come back. Consider adding the first few sights below into Tour 3. Otherwise, get to Hana first, then putter around on the way back.

Kaumahina State Wayside is an excellent stop whether or not continuing on to Hana. Shading the park are eucalyptus and numerous flora common to this part of Maui. Hike a few hundred yards to **Puohokamoa Falls** and jump in the pool at its base. Just past Kaumahina, the road cuts inland and wraps around steep 300-ft-high (90m) *pali* descending into **Honomanu Bay** (lit. shark bay) and a deep valley filled with *kukui* and African tulip trees, buttressed with 1,200-ft-high (360m) walls. The landscape is truly spectacular, but stop the car to admire, or else the cliffs and tumultuous ocean below may become viscerally interactive.

Ke'anae Peninsula, reached via a turnoff further along the road, was formed by a lava flow that came down **Ke'anae Valley** from Haleakala. At the top of Ke'anae Valley is Ko'olau Gap, a break in Haleakala's basin rim; the valley was once narrow and quite deep, but lava flows out of the gap filled in the valley and created the peninsula. Unfortunately, clouds often mask the view. Above the coast, great frigate birds with 7-ft (2m) wingspans soar on the trades. Flooded plots of cultivated taro grace the peninsula, one of the few places remaining in Hawaii to commercially grow taro, mostly by farmers of Hawaiian ancestry. Long a staple of Hawaiian society – the taro root is eaten as a tuber, or pounded into that local favorite, *poi* – taro requires considerable water for cultivation. Long ago, the god Kane created a gushing spring – Maui's first – when he drove his spear into the lava rock here.

On the peninsula, the hamlet of **Ke'anae** has but a few families, with a Congregational church ('Ihi'ihi o lehowa o na Kaua) from the 1860s and with well-tended grounds and ringed by towering coconut palms. The village used to be larger, but a tidal wave in 1946 damaged much of the village, killing several people and literally spinning the local school around on its foundations.

Back on the main highway, immediately after the turnoff leading to Ke'anae, is the ★ **Ke'anae Arboretum**, a botanical garden well worth a stop. At a tight bend in the road is the arboretum's gate, with parking on the other side of the road, the sunlight barely making it down through the

Windsurfer at Pa'ia

Kaumahina park

Ke'anae colors

Wailua and St Gabriel's Church

Botanic delights at Kahanu

monkeypod trees overhead. An easy one-mile (round-trip) path covers the garden's six acres of both native and introduced flora: painted-bark eucalyptus, bamboo, banana, ginger, heliconias, *ti*. At the upper end of the trail, alongside the small stream, are plots of cultivated taro, much as they were tended centuries ago, along with other traditional Hawaiian crops such as breadfruit.

Beyond Ke'anae, as the road climbs higher and away from the coast somewhat, a splendid overlook reveals the village of **Wailua**, flush against the coast. Flooded taro fields surround the modest hamlet, punctuated by the spire of St Gabriel's Church, one of the first churches built in this part of Maui. Between Wailua and Ke'anae, there are less than 300 residents.

The road climbs higher on Haleakala's lower slopes then parallels the coast until it reaches Hana, sneaking past numerous waterfalls that peek through the foliage upslope. Amongst all this idyllicism is **Pua'aka'a State Wayside**, offering another respite from the road's twists and turns, its pools tended by waterfalls and with the usual picnic tables and verdant flora such as heliconias and guava. For those in desperate need, possible at this point if stuck in a snaking rental-car caravan, there are toilets.

After a few more miles, a rubbery side road twists its way down to the village of **Nahiku**, now mostly ignored on this stretch of rugged and rocky coast. Poetic license permits calling Nahiku rustic, but that would be an understatement, perhaps. In the late 1890s, entrepreneurs had big plans for Nahiku: America's first rubber plantation. In fact, it produced a high-quality latex, the plantation's 26,000 trees growing quite well. But, economically, the large plantation failed within a decade. Rubber trees weren't the only dream-crop planted along the coast here. Other unsuccessful ventures around Nahiku and along the Hana Coast included cotton, vanilla beans, pineapple and sugar cane. This is all quite fortunate; otherwise, the Hana Highway would today lack its primal appeal.

'Ula'ino Road, immediately before the turnoff road to **Hana Airport** (where commuter flights land from Honolulu), leads down to the coast, across a stream on a marginal road and into **Kahanu Gardens** (National Tropical Botanical Garden). Of interest is ★ **Pi'ilanihale Heiau**, Hawaii's largest ancient temple, most likely built in the 1300s. Overgrown with vegetation until the 1970s, the *heiau* is connected with the great Pi'ilani dynasty of Mauian chiefs, probably used as both a retreat and as a healing place. Measuring 340ft (105m) by 420ft (130m), it is a massive structure, its north side facing the ocean with five step terraces rising 56ft (17m) above the base. To visit, call the Kahanu Gardens (tel: 248 8912) for hours of access.

The first road beyond the airport is the entrance to ★★ **Wai'anapanapa State Park**, an engaging place of tide pools, caves, a black-sand beach wrapping around a compact bay, and camping with full facilities, not to mention a selection of cabins – in high demand – for rent.

The most famous cave here is not along the coast of basalt cliffs and sea spires, but back in the forest: a double cave, the lower half (actually a lava tube) filled with water. At the upper end is the second cave, formed by collapse of the wall. To reach this dry second cave, one must swim through the first. Centuries ago, a local chief with a very cruel reputation killed his wife – hiding from him in the dry cave but betrayed by movement of her faithful retainer – for having a sexual affair with her brother. The water in the cave is said to run blood-red on some nights. Scientists say it is because of small shrimp living in the cave.

From Wai'anapanapa, a 3-mile-long (5km) trail follows the coast to Hana Bay, along the way tracing the old **Hoapili** or King's Trail (*see also Tour 3, page 35, and Tour 4, page 41*) This is a rugged coast sprinkled with ancient stone structures, including a heiau; expect no beaches. In the opposite direction from the park, towards the airport, several ancient grave sites line the trail.

Back on the Hana Highway, approaching ★★★ **Hana**, the road and sky both open up. Some of this land was cleared decades ago; like elsewhere in Hawaii, sugar once defined the area around Hana. But in the middle of the 20th century, it was replaced here by cattle ranching. Today, a good deal of the land in and around Hana is part of the 3,000-acre (1,200 hectares) **Hana Ranch**, one of the two largest employers here. (The large cross on the top of a hill just inland is a memorial to the founder of the ranch, Paul

Exploring the caves at Wai'anapanapa

53

Wai'anapanapa's black-sand beach

Driveway decoration in Hana

Hasegawa Store

Hana beach mania

Fagan.) The other main industry is the **Hotel Hana Maui**, on 60-acres (25 hectares) with decidedly upscale accommodations. If your money flows like the waterfalls around Hana, stay in one of the separate bungalows – ranch houses, if you will – spilling down to the wind-swept cliffs overlooking the ocean. Other than the hotel, a couple of small stores and a post office, there is also a humble museum, **Hana Cultural Center Museum** (sporadic hours), on Uakea Road. The museum exhibits the community's artifacts, of eclectic nature and background, in this former courthouse and jail, dating from the late 1870s and last used as such in the 1970s.

South of **Hana Bay** is **Ka'uiki** (lit. the glimmer), the looming, 620-ft-high (190m), tree-covered remnant of a cinder cone rising from the coast, once a home of the demigod Maui and long used as a fortress by the more mortal Mauian chiefs. Kalaniopu'u, the king of the Big Island, held it from 1754 until 1775, when Kahekili, king of Maui, defeated him. To assure that his victory was noted by others, he baked the bodies of the defeated in ovens.

Ka'uiki was later used as a defensive position by Mauian chiefs protecting their coast against the Big Island armies of Kamehameha the Great. In fact, Hana was the last holdout on Maui against Kamehameha's conquest. In a cave at Ka'uiki's base, the favorite wife of Kamehameha – Ka'ahumanu – was born, in 1768.

No doubt by now you've heard elsewhere about the famous **Hasegawa General Store**, once on the *mauka* side of the road at the far end of town, but rebuilt on the *makai* side in the early 1990s after a fire gutted the original building. The hype regarding the store, like that of the Hana Highway, is a bit much; little about the store is different from other general stores in small towns throughout Hawaii, and it's not even the only store in Hana. But it's

been around for a while, has a long tradition, and so if in need of a T-shirt or cooling drink, it's here.

The highway does a mild roller-coaster traverse across pasture lands out of Hana south towards Kipahulu. Just two miles from the Hotel Hana Maui is Haneo'o Road, which loops around to the coast for a mile before rejoining the main road. The first beach on the spur road is **Koki**. Although humble in size – there are no large beaches anywhere along the Hana Coast – the significance of the location is monumental: from here, the demigod Maui pulled up the Hawaiian Islands from the ocean with his big hook. Further along is ★ **Hamoa Beach**, a tightly bent and compact beach with blackish sand fringed with coconut palms. This is probably the area's finest swimming beach; the Hotel Hana Maui maintains facilities for its guests at Hamoa, but this beach is *not* private; it is public, as are all beaches in Hawaii.

The main road – south of Hana no longer the Hana Highway, but the Pi'ilani Highway – is increasingly narrow and potholed, the open ranch land once again surrendering to rain forest. In season, squashed mangos coat the road in places, oddly fragrant as they ferment in the tropical sun. The road arcs inland along a ravine and around a promontory with a cross nestled in the heavy growth: the grave of a Hawaiian named Helio, born in 1815, Hawaii's first Catholic and a tireless missionary. At the head of the ravine is 100-ft-high (30m) **Wailua Falls**, easy to spot both by its majesty and by the tourists. It is a classically falling waterfall amidst breadfruit and kukui trees, ending in a delightful pool at the bottom.

Wailua Falls

Two miles more is the boundary of **Haleakala National Park**. Just beyond is ★★ **'Ohe'o Gulch** (*'ohe'o* means the gathering of pools), spanned by an old stone bridge over which passes the road. Directly below are the lower series of stream-fed pools sometimes called Seven Pools, and wrongly called by tour companies the Seven 'Sacred' Pools. There are, in fact, nearly two dozen pools, and none were ever sacred. The pools are nurtured by **Pipiwai Stream**; the two large pools at the bottom, between the bridge that carries the highway over them and the ocean, are the most popular. If arriving around noon, you'll note dozens of fellow tourists who were more disciplined regarding an early start. Take care during rainy seasons, when water in the pools can be overpowering; at the overflow of the last pool into the ocean, hammerhead sharks often gather. Across the **Alenuihaha Channel** (lit. great billows smashing) is the Big Island, with snow-capped Mauna Kea. In the ancient times, the Hana-Kipahulu part of Maui often had greater political connection with the Big Island than with other parts of Maui.

Ohe'o Gulch

'Ohe'o Gulch:
ancient fishing village remains

Entering Kipahulu

Charles Lindbergh's grave

Shortly after the bridge is a parking lot, ranger station and modest visitor center. A path weaves down to the pools, skirting the remains of an ancient Hawaiian fishing village near the basalt cliffs overlooking the ocean. To the south, atop the cliffs, are several spectacularly sited unimproved campgrounds – first-come, first-serve – right on the cliffs. Sunrise from here is resplendent. Towards the mountains, another trail from near the parking lot leads to 400-ft-high (120m) **Waimoku Falls,** fed by Pipiwai Stream and upstream of the pools, descending from **Kipahulu Valley,** where 250 inches (6m) of rain fall in its rain forests.

Kipahulu Valley, in its higher reaches, was discovered only in recent years to be a sanctuary of indigenous Hawaiian flora and fauna. The Nature Conservancy bought the land in 1969, donating it to the National Park Service. Within the thick rain forest are numerous plants and birds once believed to be extinct, still alive in a precarious fight for species survival. A scientific research reserve, the upper part of the valley has been fenced off to keep out wild pigs and other feral animals – and people. Only authorized researchers are permitted to enter the upper Kipahulu Valley.

Beyond the pools and gulch, outside of the national park and along the increasingly narrow road, is the village of ★ **Kipahulu,** once the home of Laka, the deity for canoe makers. In pre-contact times, the area from Kipahulu to Hana was home to thousands of Hawaiians. More recently, Kipahulu was a sugar town from 1881 until the mid-1920s. (Note the derelict sugar mill alongside the road.) A mile beyond 'Ohe'o, at Kipahulu, a tidy road leads from the main road down towards the ocean. At the bottom is **Palapala Ho'omau Church,** dating from the late 1850s and where aviator Charles Lindbergh, who died in 1974, is buried. The site is quiet and simple, and Lindbergh's grave is not promoted for tourism – please respect the wishes of both residents and family to keep this from becoming a circus. Lindbergh, of course, flew the *Spirit of St Louis* from New York to Paris in 1927; he later retired to Hana at the urging of his good friend Sam Pryor, a retired Pan Am executive who had restored this church. The Pryors are also buried here, along with Sam's six pet gibbon apes, but on unconsecrated land.

Despite the warnings and contract restrictions of rental-car companies, it is possible to continue driving around the southern part of Maui to Upcountry. The unpaved five miles of road is just a couple of miles ahead, and Kaupo itself but six miles. When the road is wet, best not to continue onwards. But when the road is dry, scores of fellow travelers make the journey. It is an exquisite and primal part of Maui. See *Tour 4* for a description.

Tour 7

Molokai's striking coastline

Molokai *See map on page 58*

So close and yet so far. To the west of Maui, Molokai dominates the horizon. On a good day, one can see its features. Yet getting to Molokai from Maui is inconvenient, with just one flight a day between the two islands and no regular ferry. It's actually easier to get to Molokai from Honolulu, from where there are several flights a day.

Yet don't be discouraged. Molokai rewards those few who make the journey. It is geographically a dramatic island, with the world's tallest ocean cliffs, and with a history of social tragedy overcome by compassion. Molokai has the highest percentage of Native Hawaiians of any of the Hawaiian islands except privately-owned Ni'ihau, near Kauai. Unlike the other islands, tourism development has never been a priority here, with the island's economy still dominated by agriculture – at one time pineapple, but now crops such as soybeans, coffee, onions and corn. The amount of paved road on Molokai is limited, and to see many of the most spectacular sights, a four-wheel-drive is essential. Still, a trip to Molokai is one to a different, and more authentic, Hawaii.

Just 40 miles long and 10 miles wide, Molokai is comprised of three volcanoes, all small in comparison to those of the other islands. **Mauna Kamakou** is the eastern volcano and the island's highest point at 4,970ft (1,514m).

In the center of Molokai and on the southern coast, the island's main town of **Kaunakakai** is home to over half of the island's 7,000 residents. Downtown Kaunakakai doesn't move much. Down at the waterfront, a wharf extends several hundred yards out into the harbor, once used for the dispatch of pineapples.

57

Back to basics

Downtown Kaunakakai

Kaunakai resident

East out of Kaunakakai, the Kamehameha V Highway winds to Halawa, about 30 miles (50km) away on Molokai's far eastern tip. Along the way to Halawa, keep an eye on the shoreline for the 50 or so stone-walled, ancient fishponds that line the entire coast along the highway, some as old as 600 years. Molokai has the largest concentration of remaining fishponds in Hawaii, many of them restored. *Mauka* of the road and well hidden by the rich rain forest are scores of ancient *heiau*.

Near **Kawela** was the site of a battle during Kamehameha the Great's conquest of Molokai. Accounts say that his fleet of war canoes took up 4 miles (6km) of coastline when it landed. Further on is **Kamalo**, on Molokai's southernmost point and where Father Damien built St Joseph Church in 1876; the wood-frame building still stands. A mile east, just *makai* of the road, the first civilian flight from California crash-landed in 1927. Another church built in 1874 by Damien is at **Kalua'aha**, about 5 miles (8km) further along the highway.

At **Waialua**, the road winds upwards, away from the coast and into the pasture lands of the **Pu'u o Hoku Ranch** (lit. hill of stars), before descending again. Past the ranch entrance is **Kalanikaula**, a sacred grove of *kukui* trees that once encircled the residence of a powerful *kahuna*. The magic of the departed kahuna, say the locals, has not diminished, and continues to be respected.

Once the home for hundreds of Hawaiians and exceedingly beautiful, 4-mile-long ★★**Halawa Valley** marks the end of the road. West from Halawa along the northern coast is one of the world's most exquisite and dramatic sights – several 1,000-ft (300m) waterfalls cascading down the world's tallest ocean cliffs. Unfortunately, because of the setting, it is also quite difficult to experience the view except from boat or aircraft.

58

Pu'uo Hoku Ranch

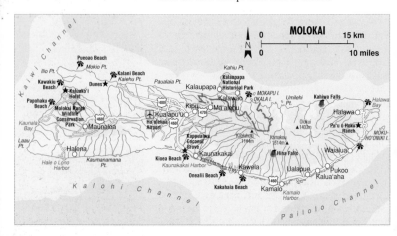

MOLOKAI

From Kaunakakai, the highway jogs due north before splitting. The left fork passes **Ho'olehua Airport** and heads into leeward or western side of Molokai, drier and lower, and where cattle roam the ranges of the 53,000-acre (21,500 hectares) **Molokai Ranch**, largest landowner on Molokai. Besides the cows, the ranch supports the deer, giraffes, zebras and antelope of the ★★ **Molokai Ranch Wildlife Conservation Park**, at the western end of the island. In addition, a unique style of accommodation – deluxe tents with all the amenities – coupled with ranch activities is offered by the ranch. ★ **Maunaloa**, a former plantation town, is a modest home to Molokai's art and kite-flying set. Right at the end of the road is Molokai's only luxury accommodation, the **Kaluako'i Hotel**.

The right fork north of Kaunakakai snakes to the northern center of Molokai. There, a spectacular view from atop 1,600-ft (500m) cliffs overlooks **Kalaupapa Peninsula** far below. Formed by lava flows from a small volcano, the peninsula is reached either by airplane, or else by hiking down a 3-mile-long (5km) trail; if not a hiker, take a mule train down to the peninsula, which is now protected as the ★★★ **Kalaupapa National Historical Park**, established in 1980, and managed by the National Park Service and the Hawaii State Department of Health. Kalaupapa is a restricted area, intended to assure the privacy of those who still live in the former leprosy colony; whether one arrives by air or on foot, arrangements for half-day, guided visits must be made through Damien Tours (tel: 567 6171); children under 16 are not allowed into Kalaupapa.

Kalaupapa welcome **59**

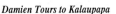

Damien Tours to Kalaupapa

Father Damien's grave

Both the geographical and historical settings of Kalaupapa are humbling. In 1866, because of its inaccessibility and isolation, Kalaupapa was chosen by the Hawaiian government for the permanent and involuntary exile of Hawaiians with leprosy. No facilities or housing were provided for the exiles, which included children taken from their families. The boat carrying them anchored offshore, and the patients were made to swim ashore with their belongings. Father Damien, who had arrived in Hawaii from Belgium in 1864, came to Kalaupapa in 1873 and turned the hellish colony into a community, building houses, a church and a clinic. Father Damien contracted the disease while on Kalaupapa, dying of it in 1889. In all, 8,000 people were forcibly exiled to Kalaupapa.

Today, the settlement of **Kalaupapa** is home to the few remaining patients once forced to live here. They stay voluntarily, as this is the only home they know. On the eastern side of the peninsula is **Kalawao**, where the original colony was located until 1888. Here is the **Siloama Church**, erected in 1871, and **St Philomena's Church**, finished a couple of years later. Father Damien was buried here, but in 1936, his remains were returned to Belgium.

Blending of Cultures

In few places does such an eclectic gathering of religions and ethnic groups live in such a confined space, and with almost no friction. The racism imbedded in human nature exists to some degree in Hawaii, and is often defined by economic status. But unlike elsewhere, people don't flaunt ethnic or cultural identity as an icon of superiority or resentment. Most important to know about Hawaii is that, on an individual level, the people of Hawaii could care less about one's skin color or religion.

When speaking of culture and ethnicity in Hawaii, one speaks of three broad sources: Native Hawaiian, Western, and immigrant cultures of the Chinese, Japanese, Koreans, Filipinos, Samoans and other groups. As would be expected, the longer an immigrant group has been in a new land, the less outwardly displayed are its traditional rituals and cultural icons. In Hawaii, the most recent groups, such as Filipinos and Samoans, still outwardly retain the ethnic richness of their homelands, whereas earlier groups like Chinese and Japanese, perhaps more confident, rely less on outward show of the home culture.

Wedding in Wailuku

61

The so-called Western culture is Hawaii's common denominator, a cohesive overlay for Hawaii's people. More subtly at work, however, and in unspoken yet unyielding terms, are the underlying currents of traditional Hawaiian culture. From the Hawaiian words that embellish everyday conversation to the many reminders of Kamehameha the Great, traditional Hawaiian ways, both ancient and since 1778, are a reminder that no one has unequivocal claims to the islands.

When the Protestant missionaries first arrived in the early 1800s, followed by the Mormons and other church groups, they did all they could to extinguish centuries-old beliefs and rituals. For the remainder of the century, it appeared that Hawaiian culture would be swept into the dustbin of memories, accelerated by a rapidly declining Native Hawaiian population. In large part, the resilient efforts of leaders like King David Kalakaua to harmonize Hawaii and the West, yet at the same time reviving the ancient traditions like hula, reversed the decline. Not only did Hawaiian culture survive attempts in the 1800s to eliminate the traditional, it has undergone a revival of the old, and a renaissance of the new.

King David Kalakaua

Traditional Hawaiian Society

Hawaii's first inhabitants arrived from the Marquesas Islands, 2,400 miles (4,000km) to the southeast in the South Pacific. Centuries later, long isolated from Polynesia, the Marquesans were forced out by newcomers from Tahiti, 2,800 miles (4,500km) due south. And still more centuries

Captain Cook

later, descendants of this second wave of immigrants greeted James Cook as an incarnation of the god Lono, in 1778.

During those centuries of isolation, society on the islands had developed in a sophisticated and hierarchical fashion, organized and disciplined in a feudal system defined by *kapu*, or taboos, maintained by the priestly *kahuna* in alliance with the *ali'i*, the aristocratic royalty. While the land abstractly belonged to the gods and was held in trust by the king, in his power was the allocation of the land's use to supporting ali'i, who in turn would allow commoners to cultivate the land. Commoners grew the food, then turned much of it over to the ali'i in return for the ali'i's protection. (As there was little of material value in Hawaiian society, an ali'i's stature and wealth was determined by the amount of food his land produced, and was often reflected in the girth of his waist.) Unlike the feudal systems of Europe or Latin America, however, the commoners were not indentured to any particular ali'i and land; they could – and did – change location and ali'i if it suited them.

Each island was divided into wedge-shaped parcels of land, extending from the ocean up into the mountain valleys. These defining units of land were the *ahupua'a*, a completely self-sustaining unit that provided fish (both from the ocean and raised in fish ponds) and produce.

Life was satisfactory and sustainable in ancient Hawaii, but it wasn't an idyllic paradise. Commoners could lose their lives if they violated sacred kapu, such as letting their shadow fall on the king's house or surfing the king's waves. And by the time Westerners arrived in the late 1700s, the islands were close to being overpopulated, a societal stress that may have led to the first migrations of Polynesians to Hawaii long before.

Votive offerings

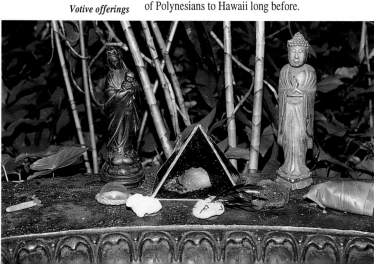

Religion and Traditional Arts

The Gods

The gods and demigods of Hawaii are those of Polynesia, brought from the South Pacific during the early migrations. These gods – and there were many – were never abstract and aloof, but integral to daily life and society.

Gods took on many forms

Gods took on many forms, including plants, and the crops from the homeland islands were carried to Hawaii by the four primary gods: taro was brought by the god Kane; *'uala*, the sweet potato, by Lono; *'ulu*, or breadfruit, by Ku; and *mai'a*, the banana, by Kanaloa. These gods each had many responsibilities. **Kane**, the prime deity, was the procreator and ancestor of all people. **Ku** was the god of war, and his image was carried by Kamehameha the Great's war canoes during his island conquests. **Lono** was the god of weather, agriculture and fertility. **Kanaloa** was god of ocean and ocean winds, and a companion of Kane.

Lower in the hierarchy were demigods like Pele, goddess of fire, and Maui, namesake of the island.

Weather in Ancient Times

While the ancient Hawaiians recognized two seasons in the islands – summer, or *kau*, and *ho'oilo*, the rainy winter season – the islands of Hawaii are rich with microclimates that are distinctive to a specific area.

Rainbows were auspicious

Obvious to ancients were the constants of rain and wind that defined not only a particular location, but also the moods and presence of the gods. (A rainbow, or *'anuenue*, for example, indicated the nearby presence of a deity.) In Hawaiian, *ua* is rain, and rain was usually named as unique to a location. Along the Hana Coast, for example, the delightful dawn rain was called *ua lani ha'a ha'a*. The possibilities for naming the wind, *makani*, were equally numerous and location-specific. The wind of Molokai was known as *Ala-hou*, for example, while the winds of Lahaina were known as *Kaua'ula*.

Chants, Hula and Hawaiian Music

Hula accompanied the chants

Long before Don Ho inflicted *Tiny Bubbles* on the world, music in the Hawaiian islands possessed a functional purpose in daily life, religion and on special occasions. Fundamental was the chant, often accompanied by drums and other percussion instruments, and which was a way of communicating and communing with the gods.

Often accompanying chants was *hula*, which performed both folk and sacred purposes by using hands, arms and body motion to reflect actions and intent. It was believed that the performance of a specific hula could influence future actions or events such as harvests. Hula was performed by both men and women, although only men were

A Hawaiian symbol

Lei have many functions

permitted to dance in *heiau,* or temples. But as the men were increasingly distracted by power struggles and politics, women took on more of the hula responsibilities.

When Kamehameha II, son of Kamehameha the Great, forced the collapse of the kapu system in 1819, the foundations of Hawaiian society began to fall apart and a religious and spiritual vacuum developed. Newly arrived Protestant missionaries quickly filled the void, replacing hula and traditional music with church choirs and hymns. By the late 1800s, Western forms of music were well established. Immigrants added their own instruments and sounds. Portuguese laborers, for example, introduced a small, four-string instrument that the Hawaiians called 'jumping flea', or *'ukulele.* Other instruments such as guitars were introduced, soon modified by Hawaiians into the distinctly Hawaiian slack-key and steel guitars, creating unique sounds and techniques that were later adopted by country-and-western musicians.

Hawaiian arts and music – particularly the hula – were revived under King Kalakaua. His sister and Hawaii's future monarch, Lili'uokalani, was an accomplished musician and composer, blending ancient Hawaiian and modern Western in a song that is perhaps Hawaii's most enduring, *Aloha 'Oe.* In Hawaiian music over the last 100 years, at least part of the lyrics are usually in Hawaiian; they tell of memories of home and lost lands.

After Hawaii was made a territory of the United States, a new form of so-called Hawaiian music – and hula – developed, but often only on the mainland; back in Hawaii, no one had ever heard of some of this music. But it took root with the American public, and as tourism slowly developed in Hawaii, musicians performing in Waikiki hotels began to blend more authentic Hawaiian music with jazz, ragtime and other mainland styles, creating a *hapa haole* (half-white) form made popular by Bing Crosby in hapa-haole classics like *Sweet Leilani* and *Blue Hawaii.*

Lei

From the time of the first people, *lei* have been important in Hawaiian religion, custom, ornamentation and dance. In ancient times, lei were gifts to the deities, worn by dancers as head wreaths as well as around the neck. Very often, the lei's material reflected the god involved; ocean gods, for example, were given lei of seaweed, called *limu kala.*

Today, lei have lost most of their sacred function, and are offered more in aloha and sentiment. There are five different styles or techniques in making lei, including braiding and twisting. Most visitors will encounter *kui lei,* common at hotels and made of pikake, ginger or plumeria threaded on a string.

Cultural Attractions

Aloha Week

Unlike Honolulu, Maui lacks the more classical forms of culture, such as non-commercial art and historical museums. In the performance arts, however, Maui has recently acquired a superb facility, the **Maui Arts and Cultural Center**, that rivals anything found elsewhere in Hawaii. The US$75 million facility, located near Kahului Harbor, opened in 1995 and covers 10 acres. Within are an art gallery, classrooms, and, most importantly, both a main theater and secondary theaters. Box office: Monday to Saturday, 1–5pm, tel: 242 7469.

The few museums that one encounters on Maui focus on missionary and whaling activities, and mostly ignore traditional Hawaiian culture. Whaling is depicted at the **Whale Center of the Pacific** and **Hale Kohola**, both at Whalers Village (9.30am–10pm), in Ka'anapali. The **Lahaina Whaling Museum** (daily, 9am–10pm) offers a superb collection of scrimshaw and artifacts from whalers.

Missionary life is preserved in Lahaina's **Baldwin Home** (daily 10am–4.30pm) and Wailuku's **Bailey House** (daily 10am–4.30pm). Plantation life is documented at the **Alexander & Baldwin Sugar Museum** in Pu'unene.

Authentic ancient and contemporary hula performances, and a 200-pound pig cooked in a traditional *imu,* make a fine evening at the **Old Lahaina Luau**, in Lahaina. For a little dust and whooping, the annual **Makawao Rodeo**, during the Fourth of July weekend, celebrates the traditional *paniolo*, or Hawaiian cowboy, life of Upcountry.

In September, **Aloha Week** festivities are state-wide and include every conceivable event and celebration, intended to bring both *kama'aina* and visitors together in aloha. Parades, coronations, exhibits, park festivals and music. Contact the Hawaii Visitors Bureau (tel: 923-1811) for exact dates and event schedules.

Alexander & Baldwin Sugar Museum

Food and Drink

Hawaii's chefs, both in hotel restaurants and at small family-run eateries, have been adventurous in blending the different foods and cuisines, fusing together the more interesting aspects of assorted specialties – Japanese, Chinese, Portuguese, Filipino, Hawaiian, Californian, Mexican, French – into what is called Hawaii Pacific Cuisine, and elsewhere referred to as Pacific Rim Cuisine, or Fusion Cuisine. And when possible, they are using Hawaii-grown produce such as Maui onions and macadamia nuts, and, not surprisingly, Hawaii's wealth of fish, such as the popular *mahimahi*.

In the plantation days, workers would bring box lunches to the fields with them, sharing with workers from other countries. Over time, variations appeared, such as *musabi*, which combines the Japanese *onigiri*, or rice ball, with that all-time favorite, Spam. No joke – Spam is big in Hawaii. Some other local favorites:

67

A common sign

bento: the original Japanese box lunch, but frequently localized. Assorted portions of rice, fish, meat, egg and vegetables.

huli huli chicken: cooked over an open broiler, huli huli chicken is often sold on weekends for group fundraisers; if you pass a smoky parking lot in a shopping center, it's probably huli huli time.

manapua: steamed Chinese meal or snack with sweet pork or vegetables inside a doughy pastry.

saimin: a bowl of Asian-style noodles, Hawaiian style. Usually wheat noodles in a broth embellished with green onions, vegetables, fishcake and maybe some meat.

plate lunch: don't leave Hawaii without eating local at least once. This carbohydrate spectacular is sold from small shops and lunch wagons. Two 'scoop rice' (not two 'scoops of rice') dished onto a plate with ice-cream scoops. Atop the rice is ladled meat, spaghetti or just about anything else that others might call leftovers. A side of macaroni salad completes the carbo rush.

pupu: Hawaiian for any sort of hors d'oeuvre, especially at a lounge or outside at sunset with drinks. Can range from chips and peanuts to satay and spring rolls.

crackseed: well-seasoned and dried papaya, mango, pumpkin and watermelon seeds.

malasada: a snack from Portugal that is a holeless donut dipped in sugar.

Thirstquencher

shave ice: not 'shaved' ice or a snow cone. Fine slivers are shaved off a large block of ice, then stuffed into a paper cone and topped with fruit syrups. A true shave ice has sweet *azuki* beans in the bottom, and vanilla ice cream, too. Most traditional general stores have them, or look for food trucks near beaches.

Restaurant selection

Restaurants are the easiest things to find on Maui, after the ocean and Haleakala. Most places are in the **La-haina–Kapalua** stretch of West Maui, or else in the **Ki-hei–Makena** strip of southwestern Maui. Not to be overlooked, however, are the towns of **Pa'ia** and **Makawao**, both of which specialize in offering casual fare that is often exceedingly good and economical.

Meet the locals

A Pacific Cafe
Azeka's II Shopping Center, Kihei, tel: 879 0069. Long known amongst Hawaii residents for its Hawaiian regional offerings on Kauai, this restaurant's new place on Maui is considerably more extravagant in its interior design, maybe too much so, but the food is that of paradise.

Casanova Italian Restaurant
1188 Makawao Avenue, Makawao, tel: 572 0220. Up in the cool air of lower Upcountry, Casanova's has long been noted for its pizza, baked in wood-fired ovens. The pasta, too, is often excellent. Casual.

David Paul's Lahaina Grill
Lahaina Inn, Lahainaluna Road, Lahaina, tel: 667 5117. This bistro-like place is elegant in ambiance, if sometimes noisy, and equally elegant with its gatherings of Southwestern and Pacific Rim cuisines.

Gerard's
Plantation Inn, Lahainaluna Road, Lahaina, tel: 661 8939. Maybe the best French restaurant in the Hawaiian Islands, Gerard's is in an old house with wonderful lanai tables. There's little to find fault with, except maybe not enough tables.

Fresh seafood at Mama's

Mama's Fish House
799 Poho Place, outside of Pa'ia, tel: 579 8488. Nestled in a coconut grove on the northern coast, Mama's Fish House has on-the-beach ambiance garnered with superbly prepared fresh seafood.

Sam Sato's
1750 Wili Pa Loop, Wailuku, tel: 244 7124. Forget any chance for ambiance and decor, but do anticipate the best of that Hawaiian favorite, saimin – well-garnished noodles in a broth – and other local snacks.

Hakone
Maui Prince Hotel, Makena, tel: 874 1111. With an emphasis on Kyoto cuisine and ambiance, though expensive, the Hakone is a trip to Kyoto without the air fare.

Activities

Hawaii always pleases. It can't help doing otherwise – staring at the ocean, windsurfing, napping by the pool, hiking through rainforests, gliding, dozing on the beach, and of course shopping. If not sure how or where these activities exist, the hotel concierge or activity desk will know. Or grab one of the free tourist magazines sprinkled in the tourist enclaves, especially in Kihei, Lahaina and Ka'anapali, and at the airport.

Shopping

Shopping around

As with food, shopping venues are clustered on **West Maui** in the Lahaina–Ka'anapali area, and in the **Kihei–Wailea** corridor. Also, for more traditional shopping pleasure, **Kahului** is Maui's commercial center.

What to buy? Only one's imagination is the limit, but before buying something excessively 'Hawaii', consider that while it may seem lyrical or delightfully beautiful here in paradise, back home it may look like the schlock that it very well could be.

69

Kona and Maui coffee: Grown on the Big Island, the Kona coffee plant was introduced from Rio de Janeiro in the early 19th century. It can grow elsewhere in Hawaii, but it thrives in the climate and soil of south Kona; no coffee is grown on Oahu, although Maui has a young but blossoming industry. Note that a blend is only 10 percent Hawaiian beans; the rest can be of generic, mysterious junk beans. If wanting the strong and unique Kona or Maui taste, get 100 percent, which will cost considerably more, but is well worth it. Settle for nothing less.

Ni'ihau shell lei: A small and dry island in the rain shadow of lush Kauai, Ni'ihau is privately owned and with but 250 Hawaiians living on it. Some of the residents collect a small, rare shell found on its beaches and string them into lei. You'll have to keep an eye open if you want to buy one of these very expensive lei, sold by the inch and found in only select galleries and shops. No, you can't go to Ni'ihau to buy one. You can't even get on the island.

Lei

Art: Lahaina in particular sprouts many galleries. Hawaii has attracted numerous artists over the decades. Some of them have original styles that have spawned scores of derivative wannabes, diluting the original artist's style so much that the work is diminished. Take, for example, the dual-perspective paintings of frolicking porpoises and reef fish underwater, moonlit waves and breaching whales above water. The technical ability of this art is superb, but one wonders what has happened to the creativity, much less the initiative, of the painters – not artists – producing this increasingly trite stuff by the truck load for the tourist market, and at excessively high prices.

Down to the beach

Access to the water is universal, as all beaches are by law accessible to everyone; there are no private beaches. Both the state and federal governments have strict and rigidly enforced laws protecting natural resources and wildlife. Basically, it is illegal to disturb or otherwise hassle marine wildlife – turtles and whales alike – in any way. Ignorance of the law is no excuse, as several visitors have learned when they found themselves in a jail cell.

The state government has also made notable efforts to ensure that water and beach activities are safe. The use of so-called thrill craft, like jet skis, is banned except in a couple of controlled areas – far from beaches and swimmers, and far from where their noise is an intrusion. Obey posted warnings and flags; at certain times of the year, beaches may be subjected to unpredictable currents – even when the waves are docile – that generate vicious undertows able to pull the unwary out to sea. Lifeguards are on duty at most beaches.

Hawaii is subject to periodic invasions of small jellyfish, bluish and about the size of a golf ball, with stinging tentacles. They usually appear about a week after a full moon, remaining a nuisance for four to five days. They hurt like hell, but aren't lethal. There will be something in daily newspapers or on the evening news alerting which beaches are affected.

Diving and snorkeling

Coral reefs tend to form late in the life of volcanic islands such as Maui, a relatively young island in Hawaii. Maui has moderate reefs, but nothing that divers would travel halfway around the world for. Nonetheless, the underwater experience is a fascinating one, with large varieties of fish. In winter, one may even hear the calls of a humpback whale here from Alaska for the winter months. All hotel activity desks can arrange dive trips.

On Maui, the most popular snorkeling spot is Molokini, a small, crescent-shaped tuff-cone island just a few miles offshore from Wailea, and thus easily accessible for a morning of snorkeling. Every morning, numerous boats carry snorkelers and divers out to Molokini for half a day of swimming in the colorful, sheltered waters.

Windsurfing

Maui is not an internationally-noted place for surfing. However, **windsurfing** does have a world-famous venue in Maui, at Hoʻokipa Beach, on the north shore east of Kahului Airport. Some of the world's best competitive windsurfers live in the area, practicing daily in Hoʻokipa's nearly perfect conditions of weather and water. Check the papers for professional competitions at Hoʻokipa.

Hiking

The 'Iao Valley in West Maui

Maui satisfies all levels of ambition and fitness. In West Maui, the Kapalua Nature Society (tel: 669 0244) offers guided hikes into the **West Maui Mountains**. Profits from the fees – which include transportation and lunch – are directed towards the preservation of the rain forests of West Maui. An area of beautiful but short hikes in the West Maui Mountains is 'Iao Valley, reached via Wailuku. Leave your car at the parking lot and take off on the marked trails for a few hours. In East Maui, excellent short hikes are at Wai'anapanapa State Park, the 'Ohe'o Gulch area of the **Haleakala National Park**, and atop Halaekala itself (for details on overnight camping in Haleakala National Park, *see Tour 5, page 49*).

71

Trekking Haleakala

For further information, contact the State Department of Land and Natural Resources (tel: 984 8109), State Division of Forestry and Wildlife (tel: 984 8100), and Haleakala National Park (tel: 572 9306).

Molokai

Molokai rancher

The neighbor island of **Molokai** is a gem with its outdoor options, but on a small scale and without the shrill competition for the tourists' attention. Some of the activities, such as the **Molokai Wagon Ride** – half a day with a locally-operated wagon ride through history and folklore – are about as down-home and local an experience as one can find.

The **Great Molokai Ranch Trail**, a lodging and recreation program of Molokai Ranch on the western end of Molokai, offers a deluxe tent on an elevated platform, with queen-size bed, solar-powered lights, hot water and private lanai to use as one's base for nearly any activity, whether horseback riding or mountain biking, horseshoeing or snorkeling. **Molokai Ranch**, Maunaloa, tel: 552 2791.

Transportation

Happy landings

The only regularly-scheduled way to arrive in Hawaii is by air. Until a few years ago, all international and mainland flights arrived and departed at Honolulu International Airport, but increasingly, non-stop flights to Kona, on the Big Island, and Kahalui, on Maui, are available from both the mainland and Asia. Over two dozen airlines serve Hawaii, mostly from North America and Asia, including United, American, Continental, Delta, TWA, Hawaiian, Air New Zealand, Canadian, China, Garuda, Japan, Korean, Philippines and Qantas. In addition, numerous charter airlines operate during peak seasons.

The modern terminal of **Kahului Airport** is located in the northern part of the central isthmus, two miles east of Kahului, Maui's largest town. From Kahului, there are frequent commuter flights to the neighbor islands, in addition to an increasing number of non-stop, direct flights from North America and Japan.

Kapalua West Maui Airport handles about 50 inter-island commuter flights a day – via Mahalo Air and Island Air. There are no flights beyond the neighbor islands from Kapalua West Maui Airport. A shuttle bus connects the airport with the Ka'anapali resort.There are no car rentals at the airport, but taxis are usually available.

Hana Airport, just outside of Hana on Maui's eastern side, is a smallish facility handling less than 10 flights a day. If staying at the Hotel Hana Maui, a shuttle ferries guests to and from the airport. There are no taxis, but Dollar handles rental cars, by advance arrangement only.

Unless arriving on a US Navy warship, an infrequent luxury cruise ship, a cargo freighter or a private yacht, there is no arrival in Hawaii by sea.

Arriving in style

By bus

There is no public bus system on Maui, although several shuttle bus companies service KahuluiAirport between Kahului Airport and Ka'anapali or Wailea.

Rental car

As there is no public transportation system on Maui, if one wants to explore Maui beyond Lahaina and the resorts, a rental car is nearly essential, unless going on a guided bus tour. Rental cars are comparatively inexpensive in Hawaii, especially if obtained in a package with a hotel or airline, including the interisland airlines. During peak seasons – summer and winter – have a reservation. Rates are per day or week, and include unlimited miles. Drivers must be at least 25 years of age, and have a valid drivers license, and if from outside the United States, an

A rental car is essential

Two-wheeled alternatives

international drivers license. If not using a credit card, expect to post a substantial cash bond. In addition to the basic rate and optional liability and collision insurance fees, there is a mandatory state $2 surcharge.

There are many rental companies, both well-known and obscure, including: **Alamo**, tel: 871 6235; **Avis**, tel: 871 7575; **Budget**, tel: 871 8811; **Dollar**, tel: 877 2731; **Hertz**, tel: 877 5167; **National**, tel: 871 8851.

Taxi

There is no uniform-looking taxi fleet on Maui. Rather, taxis range from tired station wagons to stretch limousines making an extra buck during slow periods; the fare is the same in either one. Don't expect to hail a cab on the streets, except in front of the airport. Even the hotels are shy of waiting cabs. Call ahead if one is needed. Taxis can also be hired for sightseeing tours and by the hour.

The quickest way to get a taxi is to telephone for one: **A-1**, tel: 667 5675; **Yellow Cab**, tel: 877 7000; **Alii Cab**, tel: 661 3688; **Resorts and Kaanapali**, tel: 661 5285.

On foot

Lahaina, Ka'anapali and Wailuku are very compact and walkable, whereas Kihei and Wailea are not. If not accustomed to the tropics, start early in the day or in early evening. Dehydration and heat exhaustion are possibilities if not acclimated to the weather and heat; whether thirsty or not, drink water.

Interisland travel

Inter-island flight

With so many islands in Hawaii, it is surprising to most visitors – but never to *kama'aina* – that there is no interisland ferry service. For a few years, there was a daily ferry between Maui and Molokai, but that stopped service in 1996. Two reasons for the lack of water transport: economics and rough waters in the channels.

Public transportation between the islands is only by air. On the busy routes, such as Honolulu and Kahului, there are hourly flights. Despite the convenience of schedules on major routes, there are some inconvenient links, too. For example, there is only one flight daily direct between Maui and Molokai. At any other time, one must first fly to Honolulu and make a connection.

The three interisland airlines are Hawaiian, Aloha (including Island Air), and Mahalo. If arriving at Honolulu International from elsewhere and making a connection to Maui or Molokai, you'll have to change terminals. Walk, or else take the free and frequent Wiki-Wiki Bus.

Hawaiian, tel: 838 1555/800 367 5320; Mahalo, tel: 833 5555/800 4 MAHALO; Island Air, tel: 484 2222/800 323 3345; Aloha, tel: 484 1111/800 367 5250.

Facts for the Visitor

Fresh arrivals

Visas and customs

All visa regulations applicable for international visitors to the United States apply to Hawaii. Check with the nearest American consulate or embassy. Canadians require only proof of residence, such as a driver's license.

Similarly, customs regulations are the same as at other US ports of entry: 1 liter of alcohol, 200 cigarettes and US$100 worth of gifts may be brought in duty-free. Cash exceeding the equivalent of US$10,000 must be declared.

75

Tourist information

The Hawaii Visitors Bureau (HVB), established in 1903, has numerous publications covering Hawaii, not to mention its finger on the pulse of nearly everything happening on any of the islands. The airport has several information booths and the HVB's Maui office has counter help and countless brochures and leaflets.

Touring Lahaina

Hawaii Visitors Bureau, 2270 Kalakaua Avenue, Suite 801, Waikiki, tel: 923-1811, fax: 922 8911. Office, Monday to Friday, 8.30am–4.30pm. **Maui office**: 1727 Wili Pa Loop, Wailuku, tel:244 3530, fax: 244 1337. Monday to Friday, 8am–4pm.

Offices in Vancouver, tel: (604) 669 6265; Los Angeles, tel: (213) 385 5301; New York, tel: (703) 691 1800; London, tel: (0181) 941 4009.

Sightseeing tours

There are so many sightseeing tours available in Hawaii, especially on Maui, that one might be tempted to flee the islands to avoid decisions. Tours can be booked at hotels, otherwise at the numerous 'activity centers' in Lahaina or Ka'anapali, for whatever itinerary and for whatever price range. Unless time is exceedingly short, there's usually no point in making standard sightseeing arrangements in advance. There's always room for one more, and usually cheaper.

Three of the largest tour companies are Pleasant Island Holidays, tel: 922 1515; Roberts, tel: 831 1575; and Trans-Hawaiian, 566-7420.

Currency and exchange
The US dollar is used in Hawaii. Like elsewhere in America, there are few currency exchange kiosks or bureaus outside of the international airport. All banks and hotels can change major currencies, however.

Tipping
Yes, 10 to 20 percent for restaurants and taxis. Tips for hotel porters ($1 a bag) and valet parking ($1) are expected.

Postal services

Take your pick

As part of the United States, domestic postal rates apply both within Hawaii and to and from the mainland. Likewise with international mail. Most hotels will sell stamps and mail letters and postcards.

Telephone
Area code for all of Hawaii is 808. Calls on a single island are local calls; interisland calls are long-distance toll calls, and not very cheap. To call a neighbor island, dial 1-808-number. For mainland numbers, dial 1-area code-number. For international calls, the IDD access code is 011, followed by the country code and number. Most hotels have a 75-cent to one-dollar surcharge on outside calls.

Time
Hawaii time, on all the islands, is −10 hours GMT. Hawaii has its own time zone, Hawaii Standard Time, two hours behind the West Coast, 5 hours behind New York. It is the same day as North America, one day behind Asia.

Handicapped visitors
Most hotels maintain a selection of rooms specially designed for the needs of the handicapped. Further information on facilities in Hawaii is available from the **Commission on Persons with Disabilities**, 500 Ala Moana Blvd., Suite 210, Honolulu 96813. Tel: 586 8121.
Handicapped visitor information: 586 8121

Public holidays
On the following federal holidays, all federal, state and local government offices are closed, along with banks and some businesses: New Year's Day; Martin Luther King Day (3rd Monday in January); President's Day (3rd Mon-

day in February); Memorial Day (last Monday in May); Independence Day (4 July); Labor Day (first Monday in September); Discoverers' Day (second Monday in October); Veteran's Day (11 November); Thanksgiving Day (fourth Thursday in November); Christmas.

On the following state holidays, state and local government offices are closed, along with banks: Prince Kuhio Day (6 March); King Kamehameha Day (11 June); Admission Day (third Friday in August).

Newspapers

There are two daily English-language newspapers available throughout Hawaii, *The Advertiser* (part of the Gannett/USA Today chain), in the morning, and the daily afternoon *Honolulu Star-Bulletin*, an independent paper. The daily *Maui Times* covers news and events in Maui. Mainland papers like *The Wall Street Journal*, *New York Times*, and *USA Today* are widely available, while other regional mainland and foreign newspapers are available only at larger bookstores in Honolulu.

Dress

Hawaii is not excessively humid – trade winds keep the islands refreshing – but some may find the weather a little draining.Other than a couple of top-end continental restaurants at a couple of the luxury hotels, no one need worry about a coat, and certainly not a necktie. Hawaii is casual, and for men, formal in most situations is an aloha, or Hawaiian, shirt. Topless sunbathing is illegal in Hawaii.

Health precautions

What applies to any developed country in Europe or North America applies in Hawaii. Fruits, salads and water are completely safe, and tropical concerns like malaria don't exist in Hawaii. In short, don't worry, but don't drink from streams or waterfalls. But do drink water – you lose more than you think, whether walking on the streets, swimming in the ocean, or napping on the beach.

Medical

Medical facilities are world-class with numerous clinics and hospitals. Honolulu is, in fact, the medical center for much of the Pacific community. There is no free medical care in Hawaii, and as all facilities are privately-operated, payment for all services and emergencies is required; carry medical insurance and proof of it. Most major towns on Maui have comprehensive clinics and referral services. Kahului has the major hospital.

Emergencies

For police, ambulance or fire: 911

77

Fruits are completely safe

Swimming can be dangerous

Where to Stay

Little about accommodation in Hawaii needs explanation. The closer to the beach, the more expensive and usually the more luxurious.

Bed-and-breakfast is well-established in Hawaii. Best is to use one of the referral services, located on Oahu but covering the state, to find the type of B&B that you seek. Hawaiian Islands Bed and Breakfast, tel: 261 7895, and Hawaii's Best Bed and Breakfast, tel: 885 4550.

For a vast selection of quality, mid-range hotel accommodation, contact one of the following hotel groups, who have so many properties that they can fine-tune your needs, both economically and aesthetically. Aston Resorts, 2255 Kuhio Avenue 18F, Honolulu 96815, tel: 931-1400, fax: 931-1409. Outrigger Hotels, 2375 Kuhio Avenue, Honolulu 96815, tel: 921-6650, fax: 921-6655. Hawaiiana Resorts, 1270 Ala Moana Boulevard, Honolulu 96814, tel: 526-2655, fax: 524-7993.

Ka'anapali hotel pool

78

In West Maui, hotels are concentrated in the Ka'anapali and Kapalua resorts. Most are on the beach, although condominium rentals and bed-and-breakfasts will be further inland. In between the two resort areas are countless condominium rentals. Downtown Lahaina has a couple of hotels, including some exceptional boutique-size places. Kihei, on the southwest coast, is noted for its avenues of condominium rentals, and for a few mid- to low-range hotels. Further south in Wailea, on the other hand, there is nothing but the best, with a number of deluxe hotels lining Wailea Beach. And all the way south, in Makena, is but one deluxe hotel.

Wailea Beach

Kahului has a couple of cheap hotels that nobody but businesspeople making a short trip to Kahului would consider. A hotel and some bed-and-breakfasts in Hana, and a couple of bed-and-breakfasts in Upcountry, round out the options on Maui. Here, meanwhile, are some of Maui's top hotels:

Four Seasons Resort
3900 Wailea Alanui, Wailea 96753, tel: 874 8000, fax: 874 2222. Hollywood moguls come here to decompress, and their choice is good, as there is nothing left to chance in this superbly-appointed hotel, whether considering the rooms or the fine, understated lobby.

Hotel Hana Maui
P.O. Box 8, Hana 96713, tel: 248 8211, fax: 248 7202. Less than a hundred rooms within quiet lush grounds, and some ranch-style bungalows on a dramatic ocean-side site, Hana's only hotel is about as fine as they come. If you've got the money, get one of the bungalows.

Kapalua Bay Hotel & Villas
1 Bay Drive, Lahaina 96761, tel: 669 5656, fax: 669 4694. At the northern end of West Maui, Kapalua offers both traditional hotel accomodations, and deluxe full-service apartments, all surrounded by ocean and golf courses. Nearby is the elegant Ritz-Carlton.

Lahaina Inn
127 Lahainaluna Road, Lahaina 96761, tel: 661 0577, fax: 667 9480. Originally built in the 1860s, this 12-room boutique hotel near the waterfront is filled with authentic antiques, but no televisions. Fine for couples wanting romance, especially as no children are allowed.

Plantation Inn
174 Lahainaluna Road, Lahaina 96761, tel: 667 9225, fax: 667 9293. Up the road from Front Street and the Lahaina Inn, this well-designed place is small and romantic, with a compact pool for day and Gerard's excellent French cuisine for the evening.

Silversword Inn
High in the cool air of Upcountry, this converted ranch estate house has several bed-and-breakfast rooms with fine views of both Haleakala and the West Maui Mountains. It is so quiet at night that one can hear the distant ocean sometimes.

Kaluakoi Hotel (Molokai)
P.O. Box 1977, Maunaloa 96770, tel: 552 2555, fax: 552 2821. Molokai's only full-service hotel, this low-rise (nothing taller than a coconut tree on Molokai) property is on the island's far-western shore, up against beautiful Kepuhi Beach. Full resort facilities, including golf.

Haleakala sunset

Index